KINGDOM ECONOMICS

The Mountain Within – Where Heaven and Earth Converge

Volume IV

Dianne Beattie

This book is intended for educational and inspirational purposes only. The author is not providing legal, medical, financial, or psychological advice. Readers are encouraged to seek professional counsel where appropriate.

Printed in The United States.
ISBN: 979-8-9948098-6-0

DEDICATION

To the reader who has continued this journey,

If this book has found its way into your hands, it is not by chance. The Lord has been leading you—sometimes through quiet whispers, sometimes through seasons that felt like breaking—so that what He placed within you from the beginning could finally be revealed.

This book is dedicated to the sacred process of becoming.

To the hidden seasons when God forms a life before the world ever sees the fruit. To the quiet work of surrender, the reshaping of the heart, and the courage it takes to release the identity you once carried so the one God designed can emerge.

Formation is rarely comfortable, but it is always purposeful. The same God who called you is the One who is shaping you. Every refining fire, every moment of obedience, every step taken in faith is part of the architecture He is building within you.

I dedicate these pages to the sons and daughters who are allowing God to finish what He started in them.

To those who are learning that identity is not something we achieve—it is something we receive. That authority is not seized—it is entrusted. And that the life God has written for you is greater than the one you could have imagined on your own.

May this book strengthen your resolve to remain in the process.
May it remind you that Heaven wastes nothing.
And may it help you recognize that what God is building within you will one day bless far more than your own life.

You are not lost in this story.

You are being formed by it.

And the One who began this good work in you will be faithful to complete it.

The journey continues.

TABLE OF CONTENTS

This book is for sons and daughters who are willing to be formed by God.

For those who understand that true authority is born in surrender, that identity is revealed through obedience, and that the life of Christ within us must be shaped before it can be revealed.

It is for those who are allowing the Lord to build His nature within them—so they may stand in Shalom, walk in kingdom authority without striving, and become living witnesses of His presence in the earth.

"Being confident of this very thing, that He who began a good work in you will carry it on to completion until the day of Christ Jesus."
– Philippians 1:6

ACKNOWLEDGMENTS

To my mother – your resilience, your faith, your unwavering belief that God has adventure waiting for us – lives in every page of this book. Even now, your life reminds me that only God defines our future, and that it is never too late to say yes to Him again.

To my father – your strength, your protection, your willingness to let me find my own way even when you were afraid – still shapes me. Your example taught me that authority is given to protect and empower others, not to control them. Much of what I write about kingdom sovereignty was first modeled quietly by you.

To my family – you who have stood by me through long, hidden seasons and new beginnings – I love you. Your patience, encouragement, and steadiness have been a constant shelter while this message was forming in me.

To my prayer warrior partners – words cannot express what your intercession has meant. Every revelation I received happened because you created spiritual space for it. Every time I needed to hear God's voice clearly, you had already made the way clear. You are the reason this book exists. Your faithfulness, your prayers, your willingness to war in the Spirit for breakthroughs – thank you. This book is as much yours as it is mine, and I bless you to walk in the same Shalom and sovereignty these pages describe.

Kingdom Economics Book 4 Foreword - Dr. Dave Martin

What if everything you've learned about your faith was only the beginning?

What if the knowledge you've gained, the truths you've embraced, and even the encounters you've had with God were not the destination—but the invitation into something deeper?

That is where this book meets you.

In going through the book, it became immediately clear that this is not a book written to add more information to your life. It is written to address something far more significant—the space between what we know and who we have become. Over the years, I've had the privilege of walking with many individuals through seasons of growth, transition, and refinement. One consistent theme emerges: people often carry deep truth yet struggle to live fully aligned with it.

This book steps directly into that gap.

The *Kingdom Economics* series has been building toward this moment. Foundations are laid, identity begins to awaken, and understanding starts to take shape. But Book Four marks a shift. It is no longer about seeing—it is about becoming. It is where identity is tested, where alignment becomes intentional, and where faith is no longer something we speak about, but something we walk out.

In many ways, this is where the real work begins.

If there is one thing I have observed both personally and in working with others, it is that transformation does not come from information alone. It comes through process. It comes through the moments where what we believe is pressed, where what we trust is revealed, and where what we have held onto must either be surrendered or strengthened. Book Four of this Kingdom Economics series captures this with remarkable clarity. Dianne brings insight to a journey many have experienced but have not always been able to articulate.

This book will challenge you—but not for the sake of challenge. It will invite you—but not without responsibility.

There is a refining that takes place in every life that desires to move forward in God. It is the removal of what does not belong, the uncovering of what has been hidden, and the strengthening of what is true. Often, this process feels like tension. It can feel like questions, pressure, or even resistance. Yet, these are not signs that something is wrong. They are often indicators that something is being formed.

Formation or more literally supernatural transformation is the heart of this book.

Dianne writes not from theory, but from a life that has been lived in pursuit of God over many years. What you will encounter in these pages is not simply teaching—it is experience translated into guidance. It is the kind of insight that comes from walking through the very things being described.

This is also why this book carries weight.

It is not intended for the casual reader or for the beginning stages of faith.

It is for those who have already started the journey and have come to recognize that there is more depth, more clarity, more alignment, and more purpose. It is for those who are ready to move beyond simply understanding truth into living it.

And that shift—from knowing to becoming—is where everything changes.

You may find as you read that certain areas of your life come into focus.

Patterns you had not noticed before may become clear. Questions you have carried may begin to find direction. This is part of the process.

Growth often begins with awareness, but it is completed through response.

This book provides both.

At its core, this is a book about identity—not as a concept, but as a reality to be lived. It is about removing the internal conflicts that keep us divided and stepping into a life that is whole, aligned, and grounded in truth. It is about learning to trust God not only in what we understand, but in what we are still becoming.

Perhaps most importantly, this book reminds us that the journey with God is not about striving to reach something distant. It is about returning—coming back into alignment with what has always been true, even if we have not fully walked in it yet.

That is the invitation before you.

As you read, take your time. Allow the words to settle. Pay attention not only to what you understand, but to what stirs within you. Those moments are often where the greatest transformation begins.

It has been an honor to see the heart behind this work, and I believe it will serve as a meaningful step forward for those who are ready.

The question is not whether there is more.

The question is whether you are ready to step into it.

–David Martin

Dr. David Martin
President, Dave Martin Ministries,
International Evangelist/Teacher/Mentor
https://LivingSupernaturally.com

IN SIMPLE PLAIN LANGUAGE – BECOMING THE MOUNTAIN

Who This Is For

This book is not only for preachers and intercessors. It is for founders signing payroll, managers carrying teams, teachers shaping classrooms, and creators birthing new products. When I say Bride and Ecclesia, I am talking about believers in boardrooms and Zoom calls as much as in sanctuaries. Every chapter is meant to form you as a person so that what you carry into your company, your staff, your clients, and your city looks like Jesus – not like the old systems dressed in Christian language.

The 13-Element Chapter Pattern

Every chapter in this book follows a consistent formation rhythm. This is intentional. The pattern creates trust – each chapter feels like a familiar room entered from a new door.

Element	Purpose
1. Opening Hook	A single image or sentence that arrests the reader's attention and names the chapter's core tension
2. Story Window	A modern narrative (business, family, ministry) that embodies the chapter's theme before any teaching begins
3. "What This Shows Us"	A brief bridge that names the principle the Story Window reveals
4. Scripture Deep Dive	The primary biblical text explored in its original language and context
5. Formation Matrix / Chart / Grid	A visual framework the reader can return to – a table, comparison, or structural map
6. Formation Truth	A single-sentence, memorable declaration the reader can carry forward
7. For Leaders and Owners – Reflection Box	3–5 diagnostic questions aimed specifically at marketplace leaders and business owners

8. Formation Practices	Four concrete practices for the week – Inner (thought/spirit), Bodily (physical discipline), Relational (people-facing), Leadership/Business (organizational)
9. Selah Pause(s)	1–3 moments of stillness placed at natural breaks, with a short prayer
10. Activation Prayer / Declaration	A full spoken prayer or decree the reader prays aloud to seal the chapter
11. Scripture for Meditation	2–4 verses to carry through the week
12. Challenge to the Reader	A direct, personal bridge statement that propels the reader into the next chapter

INTRODUCTION

The 490 Pattern and the Wheel Within the Wheel

The Weight of 490

When Jesus tells Peter to forgive seventy times seven, He is not giving a math lesson. He is invoking a number that already carried deep prophetic meaning throughout Scripture.

Peter asks, "Lord, how many times shall I forgive? Up to seven times?" In Jewish teaching at the time, forgiving someone three times was considered enough. Peter thought seven was extremely generous. Jesus responds: "Not seven times, but seventy times seven."

The point was not keeping score – but destroying the concept of limits on forgiveness. But Jesus rarely chooses numbers randomly.

490 Is Already a Prophetic Number

In Daniel 9, the angel Gabriel gives Daniel a prophecy of seventy sevens – literally 70 x 7 = 490. That 490-year period was given to accomplish six redemptive purposes:

1. Finish transgression
2. End sin
3. Atone for iniquity
4. Bring everlasting righteousness
5. Seal prophecy
6. Anoint the Most Holy

The measure of forgiveness equals the measure of redemption.

The Genesis Reversal

In Genesis 4:24, Lamech declares: "If Cain is avenged sevenfold, Lamech seventy-sevenfold." That is the multiplication of revenge. Jesus reverses the pattern:

Fallen Humanity	Kingdom Order
Revenge x 77	Forgiveness x 490
Violence multiplies	Mercy multiplies
Death expands	Life expands

The Kingdom replaces the economy of revenge with the economy of mercy.

The Full Redemption Architecture

Pattern	Meaning
7	Completion
70	Intensified completion
70 x 7 = 490	The full measure of redemption

When Jesus says 490, He is essentially saying: Live inside the full measure of redemption. Forgiveness becomes the daily practice of the Kingdom.

The Jubilee Connection

In Leviticus 25, God establishes a time structure for Israel: 7 days (creation rhythm), 7 years (sabbatical land rest), 7 x 7 years = 49 (cycle completion), 50th year = Jubilee. Ten Jubilee cycles = 490 years. So 490 represents a full era of restoration cycles.

The Hidden Numerical Architecture

Number	Function
7	Spiritual formation
12	Government and structure
70	Expansion to nations
144	Perfect civic order
490	Full cycle of redemption

Together they describe the maturation of God's people into a civilization.

The Wheel Within the Wheel

God's Kingdom moves in nested cycles – wheels within wheels – where personal awakening, covenant alignment, and eternal architecture turn together under the direction of His Spirit.

This imagery comes directly from the vision of Ezekiel 1, where the prophet sees heavenly movement that is multidirectional, synchronized, and entirely governed by the Spirit of God. The key phrase is: "Where the Spirit would go, they would go."

The Center – Alignment with God. Standing in the center represents alignment with God's presence and authority. Throughout Scripture the center point is where heaven and earth meet: the Holy of Holies in the tabernacle, the throne in the heavenly temple, the Lamb at the center of the city in Revelation 21–22.

The Inner Wheel – Personal Formation (Book 4). The first wheel surrounding the center represents the transformation of the individual life: awakening, repentance, refinement, covenant alignment, spiritual maturity.

The Second Wheel – Corporate Formation of the Bride (Book 5). The next wheel represents the formation of a people – covenant rhythms, unity, shared governance, spiritual authority, communal alignment.

The Third Wheel – Kingdom Architecture. The outer wheel reveals the fully formed structure of God's Kingdom. This is where the biblical pattern culminates in the city described in Revelation 21: the twelve gates, the twelve foundations, the measured city, the throne at the center.

The Anchor Statement:
Before God builds His city, He awakens His people. The Great Awakening Wheel is the mechanism of that awakening.

ONE

THE ALEPH-TAV BLUEPRINT: THE END WRITTEN INTO THE BEGINNING

There is a word in the very first sentence of the Bible that almost no English reader ever sees. You can recite it easily: "In the beginning God created the heavens and the earth." But if you could see Genesis 1:1 in Hebrew, you would notice something your translation cannot show you. Sitting between "God" and "the heavens" is a small, two-letter word with no direct English equivalent. That little word is *et* – spelled Aleph-Tav, the first and last letters of the Hebrew alphabet. Most translators call it a mere grammatical marker. Heaven does not.

Story Window – The Leader Who Ran Until the Bush

Daniel was a Christian CEO who had become the kind of story people tell at conferences. He had built a fast-growing company, spoke often about kingdom culture, and gave generously to missions. Photos of him praying with his team circled on social media. Pastors invited him to share testimonies of faith in the marketplace. From a distance, it looked like relentless obedience and blessing. Up close, it looked like a man slowly unraveling.

He was first into the office and last to leave. He answered emails at midnight for the sake of excellence. He carried his staff's crises, his clients' demands, and his investors' expectations on his own shoulders, calling it leadership. When his wife gently suggested that he was burning out, he answered with verses about diligence and not growing weary in doing good. He talked a lot about trusting God. He trusted himself to keep everything from falling apart.

Then the shaking came. A major contract fell through. A key leader resigned unexpectedly and, in the exit interview, mentioned "unsustainable pressure and the fear of letting you down." One of Daniel's children started having panic attacks that doctors quietly linked to the atmosphere at home.

On an ordinary Tuesday morning, standing in his bathroom, he felt his heart race, his chest tighten, and his vision blur. He thought he was dying. The ER called it a panic attack. His spirit recognized it as a collapse of the life he had been trying to hold together in his own hands.

On the fourth day of forced rest, angry and restless, he went for a walk. He followed a narrow trail into a patch of scrub trees and dry grass. At some point, he stopped – not because he had reached a scenic view, but because he had run out of the illusion that walking would fix what was wrong. He stood there, breathing hard, when something small caught his eye. It was nothing dramatic – just a low bush at the edge of the trail, leaves catching the afternoon light. But as he stared at it, a sentence rose in his chest with a weight he could not explain: *You are burning out. I am not.*

He froze. A second sentence followed: *You have tried to be the fire. I am the fire. I am the One who burns and is not consumed.*

For the first time, Moses' wilderness story did not feel like ancient history. It felt like commentary on his life. "Take off your sandals," the Lord had told Moses, "for the place where you are standing is holy ground." Daniel sensed a similar instruction: Lay down the tools you trust. The roles you hide in. The shoes you run with. You are standing on ground I have made holy by bringing you to the end of you.

What This Shows Us

Many Christian leaders are not running from their call into a physical desert like Moses – they are running into constant activity and calling it faithfulness. The bush still burns – not to recruit more frantic effort, but to confront the self-made pressure that is cracking us, and to invite us to take off our shoes, slow down, and let God be the One who burns without being consumed.

Scripture Deep Dive: Aleph-Tav – God's Signature in the First Sentence

In Hebrew, Aleph is the first letter. Tav is the last. Placed together, they represent the complete span of expression – the beginning and the end of every word that can be formed. So when the Spirit inspires Moses to write Genesis 1:1, God does not simply say, "In the beginning God created the heavens and the earth." He inscribes His signature into the line: *In the beginning, God created – Aleph-Tav – the heavens, and Aleph-Tav – the earth.*

Centuries later, when Jesus stands in Revelation and says, "I am the Alpha and the Omega, the First and the Last, the Beginning and the End," He is not inventing a new title. He is claiming what was hidden in the first verse. In Hebrew terms, He is saying: I am the Aleph-Tav you saw but did not see in Genesis 1:1.

Creation Was Never Separate From Redemption. Revelation speaks of the Lamb slain from the foundation of the world – a sacrifice written into God's purpose before Adam ever drew breath. The pattern is unmistakable:

- The Cross was not Plan B.
- Restoration was not a reaction to the fall.
- Redemption was embedded inside creation itself.

The Bible Moves in Patterns, Not Just in Lines. What God plants in Genesis, He harvests in Revelation:

Genesis	Revelation
Garden	City
Tree of Life	Tree restored at river's edge
Bride from Adam's side	Bride from Christ's pierced side
Light spoken into darkness	Lamb as the Light of the City

Formation Truth

The God who began the story already stands at its end. He placed His Aleph-Tav in the first sentence as a pledge that nothing in the middle can outrun His design.

For Leaders and Owners – Reflection Box

- Where have I been trying to be the fire instead of letting God be the fire?

- What part of my calling have I treated as mine to hold together rather than His to sustain?
- If God stamped my business, my family, and my future with His Aleph-Tav, what changes in how I plan this quarter?
- Where have I substituted activity for alignment?

Formation Practices This Week

- **Inner** – Read Genesis 1:1 in a study Bible that shows the Hebrew. Sit with the Aleph-Tav. Ask the Spirit: "What has been hiding in plain sight that You want me to see?"
- **Bodily** – Take one 20-minute walk this week with no phone, no podcast, no agenda. Let your body slow down enough to sense that God's presence does not require your productivity.
- **Relational** – Ask one person close to you: "Am I living like someone who trusts God with the outcome, or like someone who believes everything depends on me?"
- **Leadership/Business** – Identify one decision you have been gripping. Write it down. Place your hand over it and pray: "Lord, You are the Aleph and Tav of this situation. I release my need to control the ending."

Selah – Pause Here

Take a full breath. Set down the performance. Let the truth settle: The God who wrote Genesis 1:1 has already written the final chapter of your life. You are not improvising. You are inside a design.

Pray: "Lord, I lay down my need to control the story. You are the Author. I consent to the script You have written."

Activation Prayer

Lord Jesus, Aleph and Tav – Thank You that my life is not an accident. You were present at the beginning. You will stand at the end. You have written my days inside Your design. I surrender my idea of a fragmented story. I align with Your Aleph-Tav blueprint. Stamp my heart, my mind, my assignments with the same signature You placed on heaven and earth. Let me live as someone written into Your architecture, not as someone improvising outside of it. In Your Name, First and Last, I agree.

Scripture for Meditation

- Genesis 1:1
- Revelation 22:13 – "I am the Alpha and the Omega, the First and the Last, the Beginning and the End."
- Ephesians 1:4 – "He chose us in Him before the foundation of the world."

Challenge to the Reader

You have just seen that God's signature was pressed into the first verse of the Bible before anything else was spoken. Now the question becomes: If the ending was always in the beginning – what happened to the people who were supposed to walk with Him? In the next chapter, you will meet two men: one who walked with God before any system existed, and one who wrestled with God when every system failed. Their stories will reveal where you actually stand right now – and why that matters more than you think. Turn the page. The walk is about to begin.

TWO

WALKING, WRESTLING, AND AWAKENING: ENOCH, JOB, AND THE BRIDE IN TRANSITION

There are passages in Scripture where the rhythm is predictable. "And he died... and he died... and he died..." Then suddenly the pattern breaks. "Enoch walked with God; then he was no more, because God took him." The genealogy pauses. The drumbeat of mortality stutters. A different kind of life slips into view.

Story Window – Two Owners in the Same Storm

Elliot and Marcus ran two different companies in the same industry, in the same city, under the same economic pressure. Both loved Jesus. Both talked about kingdom business. Both were hit by the same storm.

Elliot's team had long joked that he "prayed too much." He was not flashy. But if you watched his calendar, you would see a pattern – blocks of unhurried, hidden time labeled simply "walk." He took literal walks – around his neighborhood, through a park near the office – and used them as his boardroom with God. When the storm hit, Elliot did what he always did. His prayer did not sound heroic. It sounded like decades of friendship: "You see this better than I do. Show me how to walk with You in this. I don't want to be clever – I want to be clean."

Marcus had started well. But as success came, walking turned into rushing. Quiet mornings with the Lord turned into quick podcasts on leadership. When the same storm hit, he felt it like a threat to his identity. When one of his finance managers gently raised an ethical concern, Marcus responded, "We're in warfare. Sometimes you have to do what it takes and trust God to sort it out." Under pressure, his communion with God shrank to asking for outcomes.

Months later, both companies were still standing, but the stories they told their people were very different. Elliot's team said, "We learned that walking with God is not something you pause when things get serious – it is how you survive what is serious without losing your soul." Marcus's team said, "We are trying to regain trust – with regulators, clients, and our own conscience."

What This Shows Us

Two leaders can love Jesus, face the same storm, and end up in very different places – not because of talent or luck, but because of how they walk when no one is watching. Enoch teaches us that unbroken communion in ordinary days prepares us for extraordinary pressure. Job teaches us that communion can be held onto in the fire – but if we neglect that walk, pressure will push us toward compromise instead of deeper trust.

Scripture Deep Dive: Enoch – Intimacy Before Institution

The Hebrew phrase in Genesis 5:24 is *halak et ha'Elohim* – he walked *with* God. Scripture distinguishes between:

- Walking *before* God – awareness of accountability.
- Walking *after* God – obedience and following.
- Walking *with* God – shared life.

"With" signals alignment of consciousness. Continual awareness. Relational immediacy. Interior attunement. Not distance. Not ritual. Presence. Enoch stands in the Creation layer of the Bride's formation – intimacy before structure.

Job – Communion Under Accusation

If Enoch shows unbroken communion, Job shows communion under pressure. The story begins in a heavenly court. The accuser raises a question that still haunts the Bride: "Does he fear God for nothing?" Is devotion transactional? Will trust survive when blessing is stripped away?

The turning point comes near the end. After long silence, God speaks – not with neat answers, but with overwhelming self-disclosure. Job's response distills the entire journey into one sentence: "I had heard of You by the hearing of the ear, but now my eye sees You." (Job 42:5)

Formation Matrix: Performance Spirituality vs. Presence Spirituality

Performance Spirituality	Presence Spirituality
"How did I do?"	"Where is He?"
"Did I measure up?"	"What is He saying?"
"Do I still qualify?"	"How can I stay aligned with Him?"
Identity built on output	Identity built on union
Can be controlled and measured	Can only be entered and surrendered to

Formation Truth

The church is being moved from performance spirituality into presence spirituality. Communion is not circumstantial.

For Leaders and Owners – Reflection Box

- Am I more like Elliot (walking) or Marcus (rushing) in my current season?
- When was the last time I made a significant business decision from a place of stillness rather than urgency?
- Am I closer to Job – wrestled and honest – or to Job's friends – defending systems to avoid mystery?
- What would it look like to build "walk time" into my calendar this month?

Formation Practices This Week

- **Inner** – Spend 20 minutes in silence. No worship music. No reading. Just presence. Notice what rises: anxiety, restlessness, peace. Let each one become a conversation with God.
- **Bodily** – Walk outside for 30 minutes without a device. Treat the walk as prayer – not a prayer list, but a shared presence.
- **Relational** – Ask one trusted person: "Do I seem more anchored or more anxious lately?" Listen without defending.

- **Leadership/Business** – Before your next major decision, take 24 hours of deliberate silence on the matter. Tell your team: "I need to walk this before I decide."

Selah – Pause Here

Ask the Spirit quietly: Where am I living right now?

- In Enoch's simplicity – walking with God, largely unfractured?
- In Job's storm – identity under accusation, frameworks cracking, God about to speak?
- In Job's friends – defending systems, anxious to explain, uneasy with mystery?

You are not condemned by your answer. You are invited.

Pray: "Lord, I do not want to live as Job's friend – explaining You without seeing You. Where my theology has outgrown my encounter, bring me into a Job 42 moment: 'I had heard of You, but now my eye sees You.'"

Activation Prayer

Lord, I do not want to live as a stranger to my own union with You. Where I have worn old skins of performance, give me courage to molt. Where I have feared silence, teach me to wait for Your voice. Lead me toward Enoch's simplicity – walking with You, not just working for You. In Jesus' Name, Amen.

Scripture for Meditation

- Genesis 5:24 – "Enoch walked with God; then he was no more, because God took him."
- Job 42:5 – "My ears had heard of You but now my eyes have seen You."
- Psalm 46:10 – "Be still, and know that I am God."

Challenge to the Reader

Enoch walked. Job wrestled. Both found God. But neither of them found Him through busyness. In the next chapter, we step inside a garden that most people misread as romance – and discover it is actually the architectural blueprint of the Bride's interior world. If you have ever felt exhausted by Christianity that never sits down, Chapter 3 was written for you.

THREE

HIS SECRET REST: THE KING'S GARDEN AND THE BRIDE'S INTERIOR ARCHITECTURE

There is a point in every journey where strength is not your problem – striving is. You have prayed, declared, battled, repented, fasted, and pushed. Beneath the activity, something in you is tired. Not tired of God. Tired of the version of Christianity that never seems to sit down.

Story Window – The CEO Who Said "It's Just Words"

Nathan was known for being brutally honest. He led a successful logistics company, had a sharp mind, and prided himself on cutting through nonsense. In meetings, he would say things like, "I don't sugarcoat – I just tell it like it is." When a new hire made a mistake on a client account, Nathan snapped in front of the team, "Do you even know what you're doing? This isn't kindergarten."

One day, his HR director asked for a private meeting. She placed a folder containing anonymized feedback from exit interviews: "fear," "walking on eggshells," "afraid to make a mistake," "humiliated in front of others," "I started to believe I was incompetent."

She paused, then said something he did not expect: "Nathan, do you remember the phrase your father used to speak over you when you messed up?" He froze. He did remember. *"You'll never get it right, will you?"* It had been decades, but the sentence still lived in his bones. He suddenly realized he had become to others what his father had been to him – a voice that carved identity with careless phrases.

What This Shows Us

Our tongue is never "just words." It is either building or burning, binding or freeing. In business, family, or ministry, the way we speak under pressure will either disciple people into fear and shame or into courage and clarity under God.

Scripture Deep Dive: Song of Solomon 4 as Architecture, Not Sentiment

When most people read Song of Solomon 4, they see romance language. Ancient readers see something far deeper. This chapter is architectural. The Bridegroom is not merely complimenting the Bride's appearance. He is naming her structure – her interior alignment, her perceptions, her capacity to carry weight, her ability to host His presence without collapsing.

He begins with her eyes: "You have dove's eyes within your veil." Dove's eyes are single-focused. A dove cannot look in two directions at once. The Bride's first architectural feature is not her gifting. It is her gaze.

Then He shifts images: "A garden locked is my sister, my spouse; a spring locked, a fountain sealed. Your plants are an orchard of pomegranates with pleasant fruits, henna with spikenard..."

This is not sentimental language. It is interior architecture:

- **Locked and sealed** describe boundaries and ownership.
- **Orchard and spices** describe cultivated variety and maturity.
- **Fountain and streams** describe flow.

There is a difference between a life that is a platform and a life that is a garden. A platform is where you perform for others. A garden is where the King walks in the cool of the day.

Formation Matrix: The King's Garden – Interior vs. Exterior

The Bride Sees	The King Sees
"I am dark"	"You are fair, my love – there is no flaw in you"
Keeper of everyone else's vineyard	A garden locked – owned by Him
Exhausted and exposed	A sealed spring – protected and full
Productive but unrooted	An orchard of pomegranates – cultivated maturity

Formation Truth

Song of Solomon 4 is heaven's way of saying: Your interior life is meant to be a garden God enjoys, not just a factory God uses. Rest begins when you believe that.

For Leaders and Owners – Reflection Box

- Is my interior life a garden or a factory?
- Have I allowed the King to name my architecture, or am I still arguing with His description?
- Where have I been keeping everyone else's vineyard while neglecting my own?
- What would it look like to treat my inner life as a sanctuary rather than a storage closet?

Formation Practices This Week

- **Inner** – Thought inventory with the Spirit: Take 20 minutes with a journal and write down the repetitive sentences in your mind about yourself, your team, your spouse, and your future. Ask the Holy Spirit: "Which of these are lies I've agreed with?" Draw a line through each one and write a short, truthful sentence in its place.
- **Bodily** – 24-hour speech fast from negativity: Choose one 24-hour period where you will not speak self-insults, contempt toward others, or hopeless predictions. When you catch yourself starting, stop mid-sentence and replace it with a measured, truthful statement.
- **Relational** – One honest apology: Ask the Lord to highlight one person you have wounded with your words. Go to them without defensiveness. Name specifically what you said, acknowledge the impact, and ask forgiveness without explaining it away.
- **Leadership/Business** – Language reset in one meeting: In your next team meeting, set a clear standard: "We will tell the truth here without contempt, sarcasm, or character assassination." After the meeting, ask one trusted person, "Did my words today build or burn?"

Selah – Pause Here

Take a moment and ask: *Whose face comes to mind when I think about my harshest words?* Do not rush past the discomfort. *Pray: "Jesus, I bring these moments into Your light. Wash my memories and theirs, and teach me to speak as someone who will answer for every word."*

Selah – Pause Here

Listen inwardly for the sentences you repeat about yourself – "I'm stupid," "I always fail," "I'll never change." Notice how familiar they feel. *Pray: "Lord, I renounce these agreements. Put Your words in my mouth about who I am, and teach me to agree with You."*

Activation Prayer

Jesus, my Bridegroom King – You are the Aleph and Tav, the Alpha and Omega, the One who wrote the end from the beginning. Today, I bring You my interior life – my thoughts, my nervous system, my fears, my busyness, my constant need to prove myself. I confess that I have often lived as an employee, even while calling myself a Bride. I have tried to earn what You have already given. I hear You calling me garden, fountain, sealed spring. I choose to agree with Your words over my history. Teach me Your rest. I invite Your winds – north and south – to blow upon my garden so that what You planted in me can become fragrance for You and food for others. Be at home in me. Find rest in me. I am Yours. Your garden. Your city. Your Bride. Amen.

Scripture for Meditation

- Song of Solomon 4:12 – "A garden locked is my sister, my spouse; a spring locked, a fountain sealed."
- Hebrews 4:9-10 – "There remains, therefore, a Sabbath rest for the people of God."
- Psalm 16:11 – "In Your presence is fullness of joy."

Challenge to the Reader

You have just entered the King's garden – the interior architecture of the Bride. But there is a word in Genesis that has been mistranslated for centuries, and it has quietly shaped marriages, churches, and entire cultures. In the next chapter, you will discover what God actually said when He created woman – and it will change how you see yourself, your spouse, and the Bride forever. The word is *Ezer*. And it does not mean what you think.

FOUR

EZER: THE BRIDE AS RESCUER, NOT SUBORDINATE

There is a single word that has quietly shaped marriages for generations. *Helper*. A wife is meant to be her husband's "helper." You have heard that phrase so often it can sound harmless. But if you listen closely, you can hear the weight underneath it. For many women, "helper" has meant assistant, secondary, support staff to the real calling. For many men, it has meant, "I carry the mission. She carries the errands." That is not what God said. That is not what God meant.

Story Window – The Hairline Crack No One Saw

Adrian was the kind of pastor other pastors quoted. He led a well-known church, wrote books on leadership, and consulted with Christian CEOs on kingdom culture. He also had a private world that no one saw. It did not start with scandal. It started with a hairline crack.

At first, it was small compromises that felt harmless. Late-night scrolling that drifted. A counseling appointment that went ten minutes too long. Expense reports where he rounded certain numbers. Each time, his conscience pricked him. Each time, he had a ready explanation: "I'm under unique pressure. I deserve some comfort. I'll tighten this up later."

Then came the small step over a line that moved everything. One night after a long day, he replied to a message he should have ignored. On Sundays, he preached with passion. During the week, he lived with a quiet dread. Sin does not respect platforms.

What This Shows Us

Little, private compromises never stay little – they are seeds of collapse planted in the dark. We may fool people for a season, but we never fool God – sooner or later, our heart's true architecture will be revealed, and the only safe place is early repentance before exposure does the work for us.

Scripture Deep Dive: Ezer – God's Own Word for Himself

The Hebrew word translated "helper" in Genesis 2:18 is *Ezer*. It appears twenty-one times in the Old Testament. In sixteen of those, it describes God Himself as Israel's help in desperate moments.

- "My help comes from the Lord, the Maker of heaven and earth." That word "help" is *Ezer*.
- Moses named his son Eliezer – "My God is my helper" – because the Lord rescued him from Pharaoh's sword.

Ezer is not the word you use for an intern. It is the word you cry out when you are hanging from a cliff and a rope appears. It is the word for *rescue*.

When God said, "I will make an *Ezer* for him," He was saying: I will place beside him a partner who carries My own rescuing strength into his life. She is not decoration for his calling. She is God's answer to his insufficiency.

Formation Matrix: Distorted Design vs. Original Design

When Ezer Is Misunderstood	When Ezer Is Restored
Husbands carry pressure alone	Husbands receive strength they cannot carry
Wives suppress Spirit-given discernment	Wives bring rescue to the table
Marriage staggers on one wing	Marriage reflects Christ and His Bride
Authority leaks through imbalance	Covenant flows at full capacity

Formation Truth

Ezer is not the word for an assistant. It is the word for rescue within covenant. When half the covenant design is muted, authority leaks.

For Leaders and Owners – Reflection Box

- Have I treated my spouse's (or a colleague's) discernment as competition rather than provision?

- Where in my organization is strength being suppressed because it does not fit someone's comfort?
- If the Bride is *Ezer* to creation, what does that mean for how my company enters broken places?
- Do I lead like someone who needs rescue – or like someone who believes they are the only rescuer?

Formation Practices This Week

- **Inner** – Renew how you see: Go back to Genesis 2:18. Every time you see "helper," quietly say, "rescuer... deliverer... strength beside." Let that correction wash the grooves out of your mind.
- **Bodily** – Stand up, plant your feet, and say the Ezer Declaration below out loud. Let your body feel the weight of the identity.
- **Relational** – If married, ask your spouse: "Where have I dismissed your strength?" If single, ask: "Where am I called to carry God's rescuing strength in my family, workplace, or church?"
- **Leadership/Business** – Identify where rescue is needed in your organization. Ask the Spirit to show you the "cliff" no one is talking about, and bring your strength to the table.

Selah – Pause Here

Picture the Bride – not fragile, not waiting on the sidelines, not hoping for extraction – but standing with her Bridegroom as His *Ezer* in the earth. A covenant people who carry the strength of heaven into the challenges of this generation. *Pray: "Lord, show me where my Ezer calling is being suppressed – and where it needs to surface."*

Activation Declaration

I was not created as an accessory. I was created as *Ezer* – strength beside, rescue within covenant. In my marriage, in my family, in my calling, I carry the rescuing nature of God into real places of danger and need. I do not use my strength to control. I use it to protect. I do not shrink back in false humility. I step forward in true identity. Together, we reflect the partnership of Christ and His Bride. We are not waiting to be rescued from the earth. We stand with our Bridegroom as His *Ezer* in the earth.

Scripture for Meditation

- Genesis 2:18 – "I will make a helper [*Ezer*] suitable for him."
- Psalm 121:1-2 – "My help [*Ezer*] comes from the Lord, the Maker of heaven and earth."
- Galatians 3:28 – "There is neither male nor female, for you are all one in Christ Jesus."

Challenge to the Reader

You now know who you were designed to be – not an accessory, but a rescuer carrying God's own strength. But here is the uncomfortable truth: the greatest threat to that identity is not the enemy outside. It is the quiet sins inside. In the next chapter, we will name the six silent drains that bleed out the anointing – and most of them wear respectable clothes. This chapter will confront you. And that confrontation is the kindest thing the Spirit can do before the weight of the next season arrives.

FIVE

PURITY AND HOLINESS: THE QUIET SINS THAT BLEED OUT THE ANOINTING

There is nothing casual about the anointing. It is heaven's oil on a human life. It is the Lord's fingerprint, the breath of the Spirit resting on a vessel He has chosen to carry weight in the earth. And yet the greatest danger to that anointing is not out there. It is not demons. It is not persecution. It is not critics. It is not lack of opportunity. The anointing is most often destroyed from the inside. Quietly. Respectably. Through small decisions we excuse and private habits we protect.

This chapter is not about shaming you. It is about turning the light on before something precious leaks away.

Story Window – The Company No One Could Buy

Victor had built his company from nothing. He started with a borrowed truck, a handful of clients, and a conviction that hard work plus faith would be enough. Decades later, the business was respected, profitable, and widely known in its niche. Young entrepreneurs invited him to speak. Pastors pointed to him as an example of kingdom excellence.

As he neared retirement, Victor began to talk about handing the baton. He pictured selling the company, blessing his family, and funding missions in his later years. When he casually mentioned to a few contacts that he might be open to selling, interest came quickly. That was when the crack in the story showed.

Potential buyers started asking basic questions:

- Who are your key leaders?
- Who currently runs operations day to day?

- What systems and processes do you have documented?
- What happens here if you take three months off?

Victor's answers were thin. He had managers, but every significant decision came back to him. There were processes, but most of them lived in his head. He could describe how everything worked, but very little was written, delegated, or owned by anyone else.

"When a client has a problem, who handles it?" *I do.* "When a supplier relationship gets complicated?" *I step in.* "When a high-stakes negotiation needs to be closed?" *That's me.*

The more questions they asked, the clearer it became: the business was not a transferable organism. It was an extension of one man's nervous system. One potential buyer said it gently: "We love your numbers. But we're not buying a company—we'd be buying *you.* And you're leaving."

The deals evaporated. Victor felt blindsided. He had assumed that decades of reputation and revenue would translate straight into value. Instead, he discovered that because he had kept everything revolving around himself, the company had almost no value without him.

Underneath, there was a stronghold he had never named. From early days, he had believed a sentence that sounded noble but was deeply destructive: *If I don't control everything, everything will fall apart.* That belief had quietly shaped every choice. He hired good people, then refused to trust them with real authority. He prayed for God to send leaders but kept them as assistants. He preached about body life in church while running a one-man body at work.

When someone suggested documenting processes, he waved it off as "too corporate." When others urged him to raise up a true number two, he said, "No one can do it like I do." It sounded like high standards—it was actually fear baptized as excellence.

Now, at the edge of retirement, that unexamined belief had come to collect its bill. A friend invited a consultant to sit with Victor and map the situation. The consultant listened, watched, and then said something Victor did not expect to hear in a business meeting: "We're not just dealing with a structural problem. We're dealing with a stronghold."

He explained: "A stronghold is a lie you've believed so long that it now feels like truth and shapes everything you do. You've believed, 'I am only safe when I control.' So you built a company that proves it. But that belief is not from God—and it's why you can't let go now."

The words landed harder than any financial report. Victor thought back over years of overwork, the way his family plans always revolved around his availability, the way his team flinched when he walked into a room. He remembered times the Holy Spirit had nudged him to trust someone else with a decision and he had overridden it. He had called it stewardship. Heaven called it fear.

For the first time, he saw that being the key man was not a badge of honor—it was evidence of bondage.

Untangling began with confession, not strategy. He repented—not for working hard, but for building as if the entire future depended on his control. He named out loud the sentences he had lived under: *If I don't, no one will. If I let go, they'll ruin it. People can't be trusted with what I've built.*

Then came the slow, humbling work. He started identifying leaders who had been under-trusted and over-managed. He apologized for the way he had kept them small. He invited them into real ownership: "I want you to know how this works, not just do what I say."

Over time, something surprising happened. The company became less fragile. Problems were solved without him in the room. People started thinking and leading, not just executing orders. The culture shifted from dependency to shared responsibility.

By the time a new set of potential buyers came along, they found a very different picture. There were systems. There were empowered leaders. There was a founder who could step away without everything collapsing. The valuation reflected it. So did Victor's heart.

He realized that the real miracle was not that he could sell the company—it was that God had untied a lie that had wrapped itself around his leadership for decades.

What This Shows Us

Strongholds in leaders don't always look like obvious sin—sometimes they look like heroic control that everyone praises, until it's time to let go. When God begins to untangle us, He's not just fixing a business problem. He's confronting the lie underneath—so that what we've built can outlive us, and so we can finally live as sons and daughters, not as scared owners of everything.

Scripture Deep Dive – The Six Oil Drains

1. The Anointing and the Inside War

You already know this in your spirit: the anointing is costly. It did not come cheap. It did not arrive overnight. It is the product of years of surrender, obedience, correction, tears, and yes, joy. When the Spirit rests on you in a unique way, it is not an ego boost. It is a trust. That trust can be grieved.

Scripture gives us a sobering picture in Saul. When he was small in his own eyes, the Lord anointed him as king. The oil flowed when humility and obedience were intact. But over time, something shifted. He began to edit God's instructions, protect his image, and fear people more than he feared the Lord. He still wore the title. He still led the army. But Samuel had to say the words no anointed person ever wants to hear: *"Because you have rejected the word of the Lord, He has rejected you from being king."*

That rejection did not begin with a scandal. It began with quiet inner choices.

In the same way, many of the crises we see today are not random. They are the harvest of longstanding, unaddressed inner patterns. If you lead anything—a company, a team, a classroom—your hidden life will eventually shape the culture more than your public speeches. Your people will not just inherit your vision; they will inherit your inner agreements with God or your quiet refusals.

The Spirit is not out to expose you. He is out to preserve you. So He puts His finger on the very things we are tempted to overlook. Let's name them.

2. Pride Disguised as Maturity

Pride is not always loud. It rarely walks into the room shouting. In the anointed life, pride usually arrives dressed as maturity. It sounds like:

- "I've heard this before."
- "That word is for new believers."
- "I don't really need correction anymore."
- "Accountability is for people who haven't grown up yet."

On the outside, that can look calm, composed, dignified. On the inside, something lethal is happening: the heart is closing.

Pride does not just make you arrogant. It makes you unteachable. And where heaven cannot shape the soul, the anointing begins to thin. The Spirit can flow through weak people. He can flow through broken people. He can even flow through fearful people who keep saying yes. But He will not keep pouring Himself through a heart that has decided it has nothing left to learn.

The moment you become uncorrectable, you become unsafe to carry weight.

3. Hidden Offense and Quiet Bitterness

Offense feels justified. It feels normal. It may even feel holy. *They were wrong. They hurt me. They misunderstood.* All of that may be true. But offense is not just a reaction. It is a storage system.

When you store offense instead of releasing it, it becomes:

- A shadow in the heart where the Spirit refuses to dwell.
- A filter on every word you hear.
- A lid on what you can receive.

You can sit under the strongest preaching and receive nothing, not because heaven is closed, but because bitterness has choked your sensitivity. A bitter heart cannot carry divine oil for long.

Offense says, "I forgive, but I will not forget," while replaying the scene in high definition. Offense says, "I'm moving on," while quietly building a case. Over time, the anointing does not just weaken in public. It feels distant in private. Revelation dulls. Worship flattens. Joy becomes work.

The Spirit will not force you to let go. But He will not share a throne with resentment.

4. Small Compromises and the Slow Leak

Almost no one loses the anointing in one catastrophic event. Most lose it one small compromise at a time. It starts with "harmless" decisions:

- That text you never should have continued.
- That entertainment you keep excusing.
- That half-truth you tell to avoid discomfort.
- That habit you say you have "under control."

Compromise rarely announces itself. It whispers. It suggests. It rationalizes. And what you tolerate eventually becomes what you obey.

The anointing thrives in a pure atmosphere. It suffocates in mixture. When the Spirit told you, "I want all of you," He meant your habits, your playlists, your conversations, your browser, your secret indulgences, your standards. You cannot flirt with darkness and expect the weight of glory to rest comfortably on the same life.

This is not legalism. This is oxygen. The oil requires an environment.

5. Addiction to Opinion

One of the most respected sins in ministry is the need to be liked. On the surface, it looks like kindness and flexibility. Underneath, it is bondage.

The desire to be approved, to fit, to impress, to be invited, to be celebrated—these are not neutral when you carry anointing. You cannot be Spirit-led and opinion-controlled at the same time. When applause becomes your oxygen:

- Conviction softens.
- Messages are edited.
- Hard words are delayed.
- Assignments are avoided.

People's applause can suffocate God's whisper. Saul confessed it plainly: *"I feared the people and obeyed their voice"* (1 Samuel 15:24). That is the confession of a man who traded God's word for optics.

The anointing rests on those who fear disappointing God more than they fear losing a room.

6. Fear That Masquerades as Humility

Fear is often praised as caution, but when it begins to override obedience, it becomes sin. Not because you feel afraid, but because you let fear make the final decision. Fear says:

- "I can't do that—I'm not enough."
- "I don't want to look foolish."
- "I don't want to lose control."
- "If I step out and nothing happens, I will be humiliated."

God can work with weak. He can work with shaking knees. He cannot work with refusal. The Spirit will not drag you past your "no." He waits for your "yes," even if your "yes" is trembling.

Fear kills anointing because fear kills obedience. The assignment you will not step into for three years because you are still "praying about it" might already be in the obituary of your anointing. Delay can be wisdom. It can also be disobedience in a church outfit.

7. The Hunger to Be Seen

There is a thin line between wanting to be useful and wanting to be noticed. The desire to be seen, respected, platformed, and highlighted is not just human. It is dangerous when you carry oil.

Jesus did not say, "Your Father will reward your visibility." He said, "Your Father who sees in secret will reward you openly."

Many today want the reward without the secret life. They want exposure without excavation. They want impact without hidden intercession. The anointing does not rest on the one who desires attention. It rests on the one who desires the Father.

If you want His oil, you must want His eyes more than any platform's eyes.

The Parable of the Ten Virgins and Oil Capacity

The connection between purity and anointing is not theoretical. Jesus made it concrete in the parable of the ten virgins in Matthew 25:1-13.

All ten virgins had lamps. All ten were invited. All ten identified as belonging to the wedding party. The separation happened not over identity, but over preparation—over oil capacity.

The five foolish virgins assumed their lamps would stay lit on yesterday's supply. They treated the anointing like a refillable tank that required no maintenance. They lived as though their calling guaranteed their readiness.

The five wise virgins prepared differently. They carried extra oil. Not because they were paranoid, but because they understood something about the nature of anointing: it must be tended. Oil does not replenish itself. The inner life requires daily attention—confession, intimacy, honesty before God, willingness to be corrected.

When the bridegroom was delayed, all ten virgins fell asleep. Even the wise ones. The difference was not that the wise stayed awake while the foolish slept. The difference was what they had in reserve when the moment arrived.

This is a devastating picture for the modern church. We have vast numbers of people who carry lamps—who identify as believers, who attend services, who know the language. But their oil has been leaking through unaddressed pride, unresolved offense, tolerated compromise, and unchecked fear. When the pressure moment arrives—and it will arrive—the lamp reveals what was actually inside.

The bridegroom's response to the foolish virgins is haunting: *"I do not know you"* (Matthew 25:12). Not "I don't like you." Not "You failed a test." But *I do not know you.* Relationship—intimate, personal, tested relationship—is what the oil represents.

You can carry a title. You can lead a ministry. You can run a company with Christian values on the wall. But if the inner life has been neglected—if pride has closed the door, if offense has settled into the soil, if compromise has become normal—then the lamp may look lit, but the oil is gone.

This is why the six oil drains are not minor issues. They are the very things that determine whether your lamp has substance or only appearance when the moment of testing comes.

David's Contrast: What Protected the Oil

If Saul is the picture of oil lost, David is the picture of oil preserved—even through failure.

David sinned spectacularly. His failure with Bathsheba was not a quiet compromise. It was adultery, deception, and murder. By any external measurement, David should have been disqualified permanently. Yet God called David "a man after My own heart" (Acts 13:22).

Why? Not because David's sin was less serious. But because David's response to exposure was fundamentally different from Saul's.

When the prophet Nathan confronted David with the words *"You are the man"* (2 Samuel 12:7), David did not spin. He did not explain. He did not point to his track record of faithfulness. He said five words that changed his story forever: *"I have sinned against the Lord"* (2 Samuel 12:13).

No management. No image control. No spiritual language covering the wound. Just raw, devastating honesty.

Psalm 51 is the document of that moment. It is not a worship song written for a congregation. It is the private cry of a broken man:

"Against You, You only, have I sinned and done what is evil in Your sight... Create in me a clean heart, O God, and renew a right spirit within me. Do not cast me away from Your presence, and do not take Your Holy Spirit from me."

David understood something Saul never grasped: the anointing is not protected by managing your image. The anointing is protected by keeping your heart accessible to God—even when what He finds there is ugly.

The path back from any oil drain is not perfection. It is confession. Not explanation—confession. Not a five-step recovery plan—a face-down return to the One who anointed you in the first place.

God did not pour double oil on David because David was sinless. He poured double oil on David because David's heart remained soft enough to break when confronted. That is the quality the Bride must cultivate: not perfection, but pliability. Not sinlessness, but the willingness to be found, named, and restored.

The Corporate Dimension: When a Leader's Oil Drains, Everyone Suffers

There is a dimension of this chapter that extends beyond the individual. When a leader's oil drains—when pride, offense, compromise, or fear takes root in someone who carries authority—the effect is never private.

In the Old Testament, when a king turned from the Lord, the entire nation felt the consequences. Jeroboam's idolatry didn't just affect his household; it set the pattern for generations of kings after him. Ahab's capitulation to Jezebel didn't just compromise his reign; it introduced systemic Baal worship into the national culture.

In the same way, when a business leader operates under unaddressed fear, the team absorbs anxiety. When a pastor leads from unresolved offense, the congregation mirrors bitterness. When a parent governs from control rather than trust, the children internalize that their value depends on performance.

The anointing is not just for you. It is for everyone downstream of your leadership. When the oil drains from a leader, the environment changes. Creativity dims. Trust erodes. The atmosphere shifts from life to survival.

This is why Victor's story matters so deeply. His need to control was not just a business liability—it was a spiritual stronghold that kept his team small, his company fragile, and his legacy vulnerable. When the lie was broken and the oil began to flow again, the entire organization breathed differently.

Guard the oil. Not just for yourself—but for every person, every family, every community that sits under the shade of what God has entrusted to you.

Formation Matrix – The Six Oil Drains

Oil Drain	How It Sounds	What It Costs	The Antidote
Pride	"I've heard this before"	Unteachability; closed heart	Return to "small in your own eyes"
Offense	"I forgive, but I won't forget"	Dulled revelation; blocked worship	Release; let God be the Judge
Compromise	"It's not that serious"	Contaminated atmosphere	Radical honesty; invite boundaries
Opinion Addiction	"I need them to approve"	Softened conviction; edited words	Fear God more than rooms
Fear	"I'm not enough"	Delayed obedience; buried gifts	Say "yes" while trembling
Platform Hunger	"I need to be seen"	Spilled oil; distorted motive	Return to the secret place

---

Formation Truth

This is not a private holiness project. This is Bride formation. The Bride cannot carry Crown authority while living on Saul's inner architecture. She cannot walk into the end of the age with oil in her lamp if she treats pride, offense, compromise, opinion addiction, fear, and platform hunger as small issues.

Remember: in the parable of the virgins, all ten had lamps. All ten were called virgins. All ten were set apart. The difference was not calling. It was oil capacity.

Oil is not charisma. Oil is the inner life.

- Pride drains oil.
- Offense clouds oil.
- Compromise contaminates oil.
- Opinion addiction diverts oil.
- Fear freezes oil.
- The desire to be seen spills oil on the ground.

If you want a Bride who can stand under fire without collapsing, you must allow the Spirit to address these things now, before pressure intensifies.

For Leaders & Owners – Reflection Box

For Leaders & Owners:

- Which of the six oil drains operates most quietly in your leadership?
- Where have you called control "stewardship" and fear "wisdom"?
- If a consultant walked through your organization today, would they find a transferable organism—or an extension of your nervous system?
- What would it look like to build something that outlives you—because the oil rests on the culture, not just on you?

Formation Practices

Inner Practice – Name the Drain. Ask the Holy Spirit to show you which of the six oil drains is most active in your life right now. Do not rush past His answer. Write it down. Confess it without explanation, backstory, or softening. Let it be plain: *Lord, I have been living under [pride / offense / compromise / opinion addiction / fear / platform hunger]. I repent.*

Bodily Practice – Fast from one input for seven days. Choose one source that has been feeding the drain—a social media feed, a show, a relationship dynamic, an information stream. Fast from it for one full week. Notice what surfaces in the silence. Let the emptiness become a doorway for fresh oil.

Relational Practice – Invite correction. Go to one person you trust and say: "I want to grow. Will you tell me one thing you see in me that I might be protecting instead of surrendering?" Then listen. Do not defend. Do not explain. Simply receive. This is how the anointing finds room to increase.

Leadership Practice – Delegate one thing you've been hoarding. Identify one decision, one process, or one relationship you have kept under your personal control—not because no one else can handle it, but because releasing it feels vulnerable. Hand it to a capable person this week. Write them a note: "I trust you with this. Let me know how I can support you." Then step back. Let God untie the stronghold of control one thread at a time.

The Parable of the Talents and Oil Capacity

There is an often-overlooked connection between the parable of the talents (Matthew 25:14–30) and the parable of the virgins that immediately precedes it. Both parables address the same question: *What did you do with what was entrusted to you while the Master was away?*

The virgins teach us about the inner life—oil, purity, readiness. The talents teach us about outer stewardship—multiplication, faithfulness, risk. But they share a common spine: the anointing is not just for you to enjoy. It is for you to deploy.

The servant who buried his talent was not lazy in the conventional sense. He was afraid. He said, *"I was afraid, and went and hid your talent in the ground"* (Matthew 25:25). Fear was the soil in which he buried his potential. And the master's response is devastating: *"You wicked and lazy servant"* (Matthew 25:26).

Notice: the master does not call him wicked because he sinned in some dramatic fashion. He calls him wicked because he let fear make the decision. The failure to step out—the failure to risk the anointing in obedience—was itself a form of wickedness.

This connects directly to the sixth oil drain: fear that masquerades as humility. How many assignments have you buried because stepping out felt too risky? How many gifts have you kept underground because using them might expose you to failure?

The anointing was never meant to be preserved in safety. It was meant to be spent in faith. Oil that never flows eventually goes stale. Gifts that are never exercised eventually atrophy. The Bride must learn that guarding the oil does not mean hoarding it—it means keeping it pure so it can flow freely when the moment demands.

Guard the oil. But also spend the oil. The King expects both protection and deployment.

Selah – Pause Here

Take a breath. Ask the Spirit honestly:

Where has the oil been leaking in my life—not from persecution, but from patterns I have protected?

Let Him answer without rushing. He is not out to shame you. He is out to restore the weight of what He placed on you. Sit in that kindness for a moment before you move on.

Selah – Pause Again

Think about the parable of the ten virgins. All ten had lamps. All ten had an invitation. The difference was preparation in the hidden place.

Ask: *Am I living as a wise virgin—tending the oil daily in the unseen? Or am I assuming the lamp will stay lit on yesterday's supply?*

Let the Lord recalibrate your inner posture before you step into the next chapter.

Activation Prayer / Declaration

Pray this aloud:

Father, thank You for trusting me with Your anointing. I refuse to treat it as common.

I ask You to shine Your light on every quiet sin, every hidden habit, every inner agreement that grieves Your Spirit.

Where pride has shut the door, open it again. Where offense has settled in my heart, uproot it. Where compromise has crept in, cleanse my desires. Where I have lived for opinion, deliver me from the need to be liked. Where fear has ruled my decisions, teach me to say yes even while trembling. Where I have chased visibility, return me to the secret place.

Make me small in my own eyes again, so You can trust me with greater weight.

Guard the oil on my life. Guard the oil on our homes. Guard the oil on Your Bride.

In Jesus' Name, amen.

Scripture for Meditation

- 1 Samuel 15:17-23 – Saul's rejection: obedience over sacrifice
- 1 Samuel 15:24 – "I feared the people and obeyed their voice"
- Psalm 51:4 – David's return: "Against You, You only, have I sinned"
- Matthew 25:1-13 – The parable of the ten virgins: oil capacity
- Matthew 6:6 – The Father who sees in secret
- Galatians 6:7 – "God is not mocked; whatever a man sows, he will reap"

Challenge – Before You Step Into the Next Chapter

Before you turn this page, do one concrete thing. Choose the oil drain the Spirit highlighted and write it on a card or in your journal. Place it somewhere you will see it every morning this week. Each day, pray one sentence over it: *Lord, I surrender this to You. Guard the oil.*

Do not move on as a reader. Move on as someone who has responded. The next chapter will confront what happens when appearance replaces obedience on a corporate scale. You will need clean oil to receive it.

SIX

GOD IS NOT MOCKED: WHEN APPEARANCE REPLACES OBEDIENCE

God is not mocked.

For many believers, those words sound like a threat. A warning reserved for rebels, atheists, or "people out there." But the New Testament sentence *God is not mocked* was written to the church. It is not aimed at people who deny God. It is aimed at people who honor Him with their lips while quietly bypassing His authority in practice (Galatians 6:7).

In this chapter, we are not talking about unbelief. We are talking about something far more subtle: symbolic honor with practical disregard.

Story Window – When Image Outruns Obedience

Marcus was the senior pastor of a growing church and the president of a small but influential nonprofit that trained young leaders. He was in demand at conferences, quoted on social media, and known for his insight into "what God is doing in this hour."

He also knew how to manage a room. He could cry at the right moment in a sermon, shift his tone to sound tender, and use phrases like *brokenness* and *humility* that made people feel safe around him.

Behind closed doors, another pattern had started to form. His staff lived on the edge of burnout. When they raised concerns, he would respond with, "We're in a decisive moment–don't you feel the urgency of the Spirit?" Budgets were stretched in ways that only barely stayed inside the lines, then padded with "visionary language" to keep the board comfortable. When a younger leader tried to gently challenge him about an unhealthy dynamic, he was labeled *rebellious* and quietly marginalized.

Marcus would never have said he was hiding sin. In his mind, he was carrying the pressure of the call. He still prayed, still fasted, still preached powerfully. But somewhere along the way, the gap between his public anointing and his private obedience had grown wider than he wanted to see.

One night, after a particularly charged service, he went back to his office alone. The worship had been intense, the response overwhelming. People were on their knees, tears everywhere, declarations about holiness and surrender echoing around the room. Marcus closed the door, sat down, and opened his email.

Waiting for him was a report from the finance team. It was clear, careful, and quietly alarming: the numbers didn't match the story they had been telling from the stage. Short-term decisions, "faith initiatives," and a few creative allocations had combined to create a gap that could not be spun as vision anymore.

He felt a flash of irritation. *Why would they send this now, right after such a powerful night?* "The enemy always attacks after victory," he muttered.

Then a phrase he had preached himself came back like an arrow: *What you cover with language, God will eventually uncover with light.*

He tried to shake it off. Instead, more Scripture surfaced, uninvited–Saul sparing what God told him to kill, standing in front of Samuel insisting, *"I have obeyed the voice of the Lord,"* while the bleating of sheep exposed him. The phrase *small in your own eyes* throbbed in his memory.

For the first time, the comparison stung. He saw himself in Saul–not in the headline sins, but in the way Saul loved the *appearance* of obedience. Saul wanted to keep his position with the people and still claim faithfulness before God. He negotiated around clear instructions and then threw sacrifices at the problem.

Marcus thought about the way he had used spiritual language to justify overwork, half-truths, and pressure tactics. The way he had baptized fear of losing momentum as *burden for the move of God.* The way he had assumed that if the meetings were powerful, the private architecture must be acceptable.

A second picture came, gentler but no less piercing: David alone in the field, singing to God when no one was watching. David refusing to take shortcuts with Saul's life in the cave, even when he had the perfect narrative ready– *"God delivered him into my hand."* David choosing hidden fear of the Lord over public opportunity.

Marcus realized he had admired David's songs but lived more like Saul in his decisions.

On the desk lay his Bible, still open from his message. His eyes landed on a line he had not planned to read that night but had quoted anyway, because it sounded strong from the pulpit: *God is not mocked.*

Suddenly it didn't feel like a verse for "out there." It felt like a diagnosis for "in here."

He felt the Lord's pressure, not as a threat, but as a terrifying kindness: *I am giving you a chance to step out of Saul's story and into David's. But you cannot keep My language and your shortcuts.*

The next week was the hardest of his ministry. He called an emergency meeting with the board and laid out the real numbers. He confessed the ways he had leaned on manipulation, urgency, and vague faith language instead of sober, transparent stewardship. He apologized to the younger leader he had sidelined and invited that person into the room to help rebuild healthy structures. He met with his staff and acknowledged his part in the culture of constant crisis they had been living under.

Some people were deeply relieved. Some were disappointed and left. The ministry had to slow down and scale back. But something else quietly shifted: the weight of the anointing returned with a different texture. The next time Marcus preached about holiness, it did not come from the place of a man warning them. It came from the place of a man who had chosen exposure instead of image, obedience instead of optics.

He no longer flinched when he read about Saul. He began to hope he might actually learn to live like David.

What This Shows Us

For a modern leader, being anointed in public while negotiating obedience in private is not a small tension—it is the road into Saul's story. The fear of losing image, influence, or momentum will always tempt us to cover partial obedience with spiritual language—but the Lord, in His kindness, will confront that gap so that our anointing does not destroy us.

In leadership, symbolic honor with practical disregard looks like keeping Christian language in your values while quietly letting fear of loss govern your real choices. If you will not let God's word confront how you lead and how you profit, you are training your organization to mock Him politely.

Scripture Deep Dive

1. Saul: When "Small in Your Own Eyes" Becomes Self-Preservation

The story opens with promise. Saul did not start arrogant. When Samuel reminds him of his beginning, he says: *"When you were small in your own eyes, were you not made head of the tribes of Israel? And the Lord anointed you king over Israel"* (1 Samuel 15:17).

God did not choose Saul for charisma or image. He chose him when humility and dependence were still intact. Then a shift began:

- Saul heard God's instructions clearly.
- He edited what he didn't like.
- He saved what God said to destroy.
- He wrapped disobedience in spiritual language.

When Samuel arrives, Saul's first words are: *"I have obeyed the voice of the Lord."* He has the vocabulary of obedience without the reality. That is the seed of mockery—using God's words to defend our will.

Samuel's response cuts through the performance: *"Has the Lord as great delight in burnt offerings and sacrifices, as in obeying the voice of the Lord? Behold, to obey is better than sacrifice, and to heed than the fat of rams. For rebellion is as the sin of witchcraft, and stubbornness is as iniquity and idolatry"* (1 Samuel 15:22-23).

Samuel is not exaggerating for effect. He is naming what is actually happening:

- **Witchcraft:** trying to control outcomes apart from God.
- **Rebellion:** doing the same thing while claiming God's name.

- **Stubbornness**: self-rule dressed as obedience.
- **Idolatry**: placing our judgment above His.

Saul's confession finally surfaces: *"I feared the people and obeyed their voice"* (1 Samuel 15:24). Fear did not make him panic. Fear made him selective. He chose optics over obedience. He kept his calling and quietly set aside God's command. That is how mockery begins.

2. What "God Is Not Mocked" Actually Means

When Paul writes, *"Do not be deceived: God is not mocked, for whatever a man sows, that he will also reap,"* he uses a word that means to turn up the nose, to sneer (Galatians 6:7).

Mocking God is not primarily about laughing at Him. It is about living as if His order can be bypassed while we keep using His language:

- Saying "Lord, Lord" but refusing to do what He says.
- Keeping the sacrifices, songs, and titles while cutting around the inconvenient commands.
- Assuming that because nothing collapsed last time, nothing will collapse at all.

God is not mocked means this: spiritual reality cannot be indefinitely overridden by performance. The law of sowing and reaping will stand even if we quote verses over our fields.

Saul wanted the benefits of the anointing along with the freedom to adjust God's word as needed. That combination is lethal. Samuel completes the sentence many skip: *"Because you have rejected the word of the Lord, He has also rejected you from being king"* (1 Samuel 15:23).

Notice the sequence:

1. Saul rejects the word.
2. Then God rejects Saul's role.

God does not abandon Saul as a human being. He withdraws His support from Saul's authority. He will not empower what openly contradicts Him.

3. How Mockery Grows Quietly in the Church

Mockery rarely looks like open defiance at first. It looks like:

- **Partial obedience –** doing enough to look compliant.
- **Delayed obedience –** "not yet," "the people aren't ready," "timing."
- **Reframed obedience –** using religious language to justify the opposite of what God said.
- **Selective hearing –** embracing words that affirm us and ignoring words that confront us.

We begin to sow:

- Sermons without surrender.
- Strategies without listening.
- Public honor for God without private submission to Him.

And then we are bewildered when we reap:

- Loss of authority.
- Confusion in leadership.
- Exposure of hidden patterns.
- A sense that heaven's weight has lifted, even while activity remains high.

We call it "attack." We call it "warfare." Sometimes it is simply Galatians 6:7 coming due. *God is not mocked* is not God lashing out. It is spiritual law refusing to be edited.

4. Romans 8: Flesh Religion vs. Spirit Sonship

Romans 8 explains the inner engine driving stories like Saul's: *"The mind set on the flesh is death... it does not submit to the law of God... those who are in the flesh cannot please God"* (Romans 8:6–8).

The flesh here is not just obvious sin. It is any system where self sits in the decision seat—where we remain in charge, even while we use spiritual language. That is why rebellion and witchcraft share the same root. Witchcraft seeks control apart from God. Flesh seeks autonomy apart from God. Different costume, same core.

Saul governed from the flesh:

- He knew the word.
- He modified it.
- He justified the modification.
- He used the people as his reason.

David sinned badly in visible ways, yet he was never discarded the way Saul was. Why? Because David's core posture was not self-rule. When confronted, he collapsed before God: *"Against You, You only, have I sinned"* (Psalm 51:4). He did not manage the optics. He returned.

Romans 8 calls that posture sonship: *"For as many as are led by the Spirit of God, these are sons of God"* (Romans 8:14).

- Saul clung to position while resisting the word.
- David surrendered position and threw himself on the word.

God does not reject sons. But He will remove authority from those who persist in using His name to protect their own will.

5. Why This Is Crisis Language for Our Time

If you look honestly at much of modern church culture, you will see Saul's pattern wearing contemporary clothes:

- We say "Grace," but sometimes mean, "God will keep blessing my disobedience."
- We say "No condemnation," but sometimes mean, "No consequences."
- We say "God understands my heart," while ignoring the very thing He clearly spoke.

Here is the honest tension:

- The gospel announces: *"There is therefore now no condemnation for those who are in Christ Jesus"* (Romans 8:1).
- The same gospel says: *"Whatever a man sows, that he will also reap"* (Galatians 6:7).

There is no contradiction. *No condemnation* means God does not hold your forgiven sins against you in judgment. *Sowing and reaping* means He will not endorse patterns that destroy you, even if you quote verses over them.

Grace does not suspend reality. Grace makes it possible to realign with it. *God is not mocked* is actually good news. It means reality is stable enough that repentance still works.

---

6. How the Bride Responds

The point of this chapter is not to leave you in dread. It is to bring the Bride back into alignment before the weight of the next season rests on her shoulders.

A Bride prepared to reign cannot live on:

- Half-obedience
- Carefully managed image
- Opinion addiction
- Flesh-based leadership wrapped in spiritual phrases

She must become a people who tremble again at His word.

What does that look like in real life?

Let God's word cut through your explanations. Ask Him plainly: *Where have I edited what You said? Where have I used spiritual language to cover disobedience?* Then listen, without rushing to soften what He shows.

Return to small in your own eyes. Not as a posture of groveling—but as an honest recalibration of who is actually in charge. The anointing flourishes where a heart trembles at God's Word. It withers where a heart has become its own authority.

Choose David's pattern over Saul's. When exposed, do not manage. Return. When confronted, do not spin. Confess. When afraid, do not retreat into image. Fall on your face and say, *"You are right."*

Let the sowing and reaping principle work for you, not against you. Galatians 6:7 is not only a warning—it is a promise. If you sow honesty, you will reap trust. If you sow obedience, you will reap authority. If you sow humility, you will reap promotion from God's hand rather than your own.

The Ananias and Sapphira Warning for Modern Leaders

The story of Ananias and Sapphira in Acts 5 functions as a direct application of "God is not mocked" within the early church.

They sold property. They brought a portion to the apostles. No one required them to sell. No one dictated the amount. Their sin was not stinginess—it was performance. They claimed the partial was the whole. They wanted the reputation of radical generosity without the reality.

Peter's words cut to the center: *"You have not lied to men, but to God"* (Acts 5:4).

This story is uncomfortable because it happened inside a Spirit-filled community. Not among pagans. Not among religious outsiders. Among believers who had witnessed Pentecost, who had seen the lame walk and the dead raised. And still, the temptation to perform rather than surrender proved deadly.

For modern leaders, the Ananias-and-Sapphira warning is not about money. It is about the gap between what we present and what is true. Every time we:

- Present a cleaned-up version of our finances to the board
- Frame a failure as "God redirecting" when it was actually negligence

- Use testimonial language to describe results that were manufactured
- Claim spiritual authority for decisions driven by personal ambition

...we are walking on the same ground where Ananias and Sapphira fell.

The severity of their judgment was not because God is cruel. It was because the early church was in its infancy and could not survive being built on a foundation of pretense. If performance was allowed to root itself in the foundation, everything built on top would be compromised.

The same is true of your organization, your family, and your ministry. The foundation determines the building. If the foundation is performance—spiritual language covering practical dishonesty—then every floor added above will eventually crack.

The Grace That Makes Honesty Safe

Here is the good news hidden inside the severity: God's confrontation is always an invitation to freedom.

Marcus discovered this. When he finally told the truth to his board, some people left. But the ones who stayed built something real. The anointing returned with a different texture—heavier, more honest, less polished, more powerful.

This is the paradox of grace: the very thing you fear—exposure—is the thing that releases you. As long as the gap between your vocabulary and your obedience remains hidden, it controls you. The moment it is brought into the light, it loses its power.

Grace does not excuse the gap. Grace makes it safe to close it.

"If we confess our sins, He is faithful and just to forgive us our sins and to cleanse us from all unrighteousness" (1 John 1:9).

Notice: faithful *and just.* Forgiveness is not God bending the rules. It is God operating within His own righteous system—a system where the blood of Jesus has already satisfied every charge. You are not asking God to overlook something. You are stepping into what Christ has already purchased.

That is why "God is not mocked" is actually good news. It means reality is stable enough that repentance still works. It means the law of sowing and reaping guarantees that if you sow honesty now, you will reap restoration later.

The Bride does not mock God. The Bride returns to Him—openly, honestly, without management—and discovers that His arms were open the entire time.

Formation Matrix – Saul vs. David: Two Responses to Exposure

Dimension	Saul's Pattern	David's Pattern
When confronted	"I have obeyed the Lord" – defended	"Against You only have I sinned" – surrendered
Core posture	Self-preservation	Self-surrender
Relationship to people	"I feared the people" – opinion-driven	Worshipped alone in the field – God-driven
Response to failure	Managed the optics	Fell on his face
Language	Vocabulary of obedience; heart of refusal	Broken confession; heart of return
Outcome	Anointing lifted; authority removed	Anointing doubled; covenant endured

---

Formation Truth

The Bride cannot carry Crown authority while operating on Saul's software. Saul-pattern leadership looks impressive from the outside—titles, activity, crowds—but it is a structure built on self-rule baptized in spiritual language. David-pattern leadership looks messier, more honest, more vulnerable—but it is the only architecture that can carry the weight of the age to come.

The Spirit is searching the churches today the same way He searched them in Revelation 2-3: *"I know your works."* The question is not whether you are busy. The question is whether your obedience matches your vocabulary.

For Leaders & Owners – Reflection Box

For Leaders & Owners:

- Where has "vision" language covered decisions that were really driven by fear of loss?
- If God sent a Samuel into your boardroom today with the question, "What is this bleating of sheep I hear?"—what would the bleating be?
- Are there people on your team who have tried to speak truth and been labeled "rebellious"?
- What would change in your organization if obedience—not optics—became the standard?

Formation Practices

Inner Practice – The Saul Audit. Sit quietly with the Lord and ask: *Where have I used spiritual language to cover disobedience?* Write down anything that surfaces. Do not explain it, defend it, or give it a backstory. Simply confess it: *Lord, this is what I have done. I return to You.*

Bodily Practice – A day of silence. Choose one day this week to refrain from posting, sharing, or performing spiritually in any public way. No social media declarations, no impressive prayers in front of others. Just you and God, hidden. Let your body remember what obedience feels like without an audience.

Relational Practice – Restore a voice you silenced. Think of one person who tried to bring truth to you and was shut down, ignored, or marginalized. Reach out. You do not have to agree with everything they said. But you can say: "I realize I did not receive you well. I want to learn to listen better. Will you tell me what you saw?"

Leadership Practice – Transparency test. Bring one area of your leadership into the light this week—a financial report that has been vague, a culture issue that has been excused, a pattern that has been covered in "faith language." Share it with at least one trustworthy person and ask: "Am I being honest about this, or am I managing the narrative?"

---

7. The Corporate Test: Saul's Pattern in Modern Institutions

Saul's pattern does not only show up in individual lives. It shows up in institutional cultures—churches, businesses, ministries, and nonprofits that have adopted the form of obedience while quietly operating from a different center.

Consider the markers:

The mission statement says one thing; the budget says another. A church proclaims "reaching the lost" while spending 90% of its budget on internal comfort. A business claims "employee well-being" while structuring compensation to extract maximum output at minimum investment. The words on the wall do not match the numbers in the spreadsheet. That is institutional mockery.

Spiritual authority is used to suppress honest questions. When a leader says "God told me" and no one is permitted to ask "How do you know?"—that is Saul's operating system running at the organizational level. Divine guidance becomes an unquestionable trump card that serves the leader's preferences rather than the community's discernment.

Success metrics replace obedience metrics. When growth, revenue, attendance, and influence become the primary measures of health—and when anyone who asks "But are we obedient?" is treated as a killjoy—the institution has crossed from faith into Saul's territory. Saul's army was impressive. His victories were real. But the bleating of the sheep exposed that the victories were built on negotiated obedience.

Turnover is explained away instead of examined. When good people keep leaving and the institutional explanation is always "they couldn't handle the vision" or "they weren't really called"—a Saul pattern is likely present. In a healthy culture, departure prompts self-examination. In a Saul culture, departure is always the other person's failure.

The remedy is not to become paranoid about institutional sin. The remedy is to create structures of accountability—regular external review, genuine board governance, anonymous feedback mechanisms, and leaders who actively invite the kind of confrontation that Samuel brought to Saul.

The institution that fears exposure more than it fears God is already operating on Saul's software, no matter how many worship songs it sings.

8. The Path from Saul to David: Three Practical Shifts

For the leader who recognizes Saul's pattern in themselves, three practical shifts begin the journey toward David's posture:

Shift 1: From managing to confessing. When something goes wrong, your first instinct will be to manage the narrative—explain, contextualize, spin. David's instinct was different: *"I have sinned against the Lord."* Full stop. No management. Practice saying those words without any follow-up explanation. Let them stand alone. The Holy Spirit will do more through raw confession than your most eloquent explanation could ever achieve.

Shift 2: From opinion-driven to Word-driven. Saul feared the people and obeyed their voice. David feared the Lord and obeyed His Word—even when the people didn't understand. This means making decisions that may confuse your team, your board, or your congregation, because God has spoken. It means letting Scripture evaluate your strategy rather than using strategy to reinterpret Scripture.

Shift 3: From positional to relational. Saul clung to his title even after the anointing departed. David's identity was never in his position—it was in his relationship with God. When you start protecting your role more than your intimacy with God, you have crossed the line. The question is not "Am I still in charge?" The question is "Am I still connected?"

These shifts are not one-time events. They are daily practices. Every morning, the Saul instinct and the David instinct compete for the driver's seat. The Bride is formed by the daily choice to let David's posture win.

Selah – Pause Here

Saul's confession was six words: *"I feared the people and obeyed their voice."*

Ask yourself: *Whose voice am I obeying—God's, or the room's?*

Sit with that question. Let it do its work. The Spirit is not trying to humiliate you. He is trying to save you from building a life that looks like a kingdom but operates like a brand.

Selah – Pause Again

David did not become "a man after God's own heart" because he never sinned. He became that man because when he was caught, he did not run, spin, or manage. He returned.

Ask: *When was the last time I truly returned to God—not managed the situation, not reframed the narrative, but simply fell on my face and said, "You are right"?*

If it has been a while, today can be that day.

Activation Prayer / Declaration

Pray this aloud:

Father, I do not want to mock You with my mouth while my life tells a different story.

I repent for every place I have used spiritual language to cover disobedience. I repent for partial obedience that kept the parts of Your word I liked and edited the parts I didn't.

I do not want to be Saul—holding a title while losing Your presence. I want to be David—losing face if necessary, but never losing You.

Search me, O God. Know my heart. Test me and know my anxious thoughts. See if there is any offensive way in me, and lead me in the way everlasting.

Restore the fear of the Lord in my life. Not dread—but holy reverence that values Your word above my comfort, Your truth above my image, and Your presence above my platform.

I choose obedience over sacrifice. I choose honesty over optics. I choose return over management.

In Jesus' Name, amen.

Scripture for Meditation

- 1 Samuel 15:17-24 – Saul's tragic arc: from small in his own eyes to rejected
- Galatians 6:7 – "God is not mocked; whatever a man sows, he will also reap"
- Romans 8:5-14 – Flesh vs. Spirit; sonship through being Spirit-led
- Psalm 51:1-4 – David's model of return
- Psalm 139:23-24 – "Search me, O God, and know my heart"

Challenge – Before You Step Into the Next Chapter

Write down one area where your vocabulary has outpaced your obedience. Be specific. Then take one step of alignment before you read another word. That step might be a phone call, a confession, a financial correction, or a conversation you have been postponing.

God is not mocked. But He is merciful. And His mercy makes it safe to stop pretending.

The next chapter traces mockery across the full arc of Scripture—from Eden to the modern church—so you can see that this pattern is not new, and neither is God's remedy.

SEVEN

THE TRACE OF MOCKERY: FROM EDEN TO THE MODERN CHURCH

Mockery did not begin with Galatians. It began in a garden. The pattern of honoring God's words while quietly editing His authority has been weaving through human history since the first conversation between a serpent and a woman. If you can trace the thread, you can recognize it when it shows up in your own mirror.

This chapter follows the mockery trace from Eden through Israel, through the prophets, through the first-century church, and into the patterns we see today—so you can see that what feels modern is actually ancient, and what feels personal is actually systemic.

Story Window – The Board Meeting No One Talks About

Denise served on the elder board of a well-known church for eleven years. She was respected, experienced, and deeply devoted to the congregation. But over time, she noticed a pattern in how the board operated.

Whenever the senior pastor brought a proposal, the board approved it. Not after discussion. Not after prayerful deliberation. After a brief spiritual moment—someone would read a verse, someone would pray—and then the vote would come. Unanimously. Every time.

The few times Denise raised a question, something subtle happened. The room didn't argue with her. It absorbed her. "That's a great point, Denise. Let's put a pin in it and revisit." They never revisited. Her concern would be logged in the minutes and buried under momentum.

One evening, the pastor proposed a multimillion-dollar building expansion. The presentation was slick—renderings, projections, a capital campaign timeline. But the giving data didn't support the vision. The church was already stretched. Several families had left over theological concerns, and giving had plateaued.

Denise said, quietly and respectfully, "I think we need to slow down. The numbers don't match the narrative. And I'm not sure this is the Lord's timing."

The room went silent. Then the pastor smiled and said, "Denise, I hear you. But sometimes faith requires us to move beyond what the numbers say. That's what faith is."

She recognized the move. It was the same spiritual language she had seen cover financial gaps, staffing decisions, and cultural drift for over a decade. *Faith* had become the override code—the word that shut down any conversation the leadership didn't want to have.

That night at home, she opened her Bible to 1 Samuel 15 and read the story of Saul again. A sentence jumped out: *"I feared the people and obeyed their voice."*

She thought about the board. No one on that board feared God more than they feared the pastor's disappointment. Including, she realized with a sharp sting, herself.

Over the next month, Denise wrote a careful, honest letter to the board—naming the pattern, citing specific examples, and asking for an independent financial review. She sent it with trembling hands.

The response was swift. A private meeting. A "concern for her heart." A suggestion that perhaps she was burned out and needed a season of rest. Within three months, she was off the board.

But something had shifted. Two other board members, reading her letter in private, began asking their own questions. One requested the full financial records. Another opened a conversation with the staff about the culture of unquestioned agreement.

The building expansion was quietly shelved six months later. No announcement. No acknowledgment. Just a pivot to a new "season of consolidation."

Denise never received an apology. But she also never regretted speaking.

What This Shows Us

Mockery doesn't always roar. Sometimes it governs through a board meeting where spiritual language replaces honest evaluation. When faith becomes a tool for silencing questions, the spirit of Saul is running the room—even if the people in it love Jesus deeply. The Bride must learn to discern when "faith language" is being used to protect the leader's will rather than to follow the Lord's.

Scripture Deep Dive – The Mockery Trace Timeline

1. Eden: The First Edit

The serpent's strategy was not to deny God's word. It was to edit it.

"Did God really say...?" (Genesis 3:1).

That question did not reject God. It reframed Him. It suggested that His word could be interpreted differently—that obedience was optional when the fruit looked good, promised wisdom, and felt right. The woman saw that the tree was good for food, pleasant to the eyes, and desirable to make one wise. Three appeals. Three overrides of a single, clear command.

Eden's mockery was not atheism. It was theology with a different conclusion. And that is always the most dangerous form.

2. Israel at Sinai: Fast Agreement, Faster Betrayal

At the base of the mountain, Israel said the words: *"All that the Lord has spoken we will do"* (Exodus 19:8). Within weeks, they built a golden calf and declared, *"These are your gods, O Israel, who brought you up out of Egypt"* (Exodus 32:4).

They did not abandon religion. They replaced its object. They kept the worship language and redirected it toward something they could see, touch, and control. That is mockery in a liturgical robe—keeping the form while gutting the substance.

The pattern continues through the entire period of the Judges: cycles of covenant, compromise, collapse, and crying out. Each generation honored God's rescue with its mouth and returned to its own ways with its feet.

3. The Prophets: Confronting Religious Performance

Isaiah delivered God's indictment: *"These people draw near with their mouths and honor Me with their lips, but have removed their hearts far from Me"* (Isaiah 29:13).

Amos thundered: *"I hate, I despise your feast days... Take away from Me the noise of your songs... But let justice run down like water, and righteousness like a mighty stream"* (Amos 5:21-24).

Malachi confronted priests who offered blind, lame, and sick animals—keeping the form of sacrifice while dishonoring its substance: *"Try offering that to your governor! Would he be pleased with you?"* (Malachi 1:8).

The prophets were not angry at pagans. They were angry at the covenant people who had perfected the art of religious appearance without relational obedience.

4. Jesus: The Sharpest Diagnosis

Jesus reserved His harshest words not for sinners, tax collectors, or Romans—but for religious leaders. He called the Pharisees whitewashed tombs, blind guides, and children of those who killed the prophets.

His core charge: *"You tithe mint and dill and cumin, and have neglected the weightier matters of the law—justice, mercy, and faithfulness"* (Matthew 23:23).

They had the measurements right but the heart wrong. They had perfected obedience to the visible while abandoning obedience to the relational. That is mockery at its most refined: accurate theology serving a disobedient heart.

5. The Early Church: Ananias and Sapphira

In Acts 5, a couple sold property and brought a portion of the proceeds to the apostles—claiming it was the full amount. No one forced them to sell. No one required a certain gift. Their sin was not in the amount. Their sin was in the lie.

Peter's words reveal the depth of the issue: *"You have not lied to men, but to God"* (Acts 5:4).

They wanted the reputation of radical generosity without the reality. It was image management inside a Spirit-filled community. And the consequence was immediate—not because God was harsh, but because the infant church could not afford to build on a foundation of performance.

6. The Modern Church: The Pattern Returns

Today, the mockery trace continues in recognizable forms:

- Churches that preach generosity while operating in financial opacity.
- Leaders who teach servanthood while demanding unquestioned loyalty.
- Conferences that celebrate revival while tolerating abuse behind the scenes.
- Congregations that speak boldly about holiness on Sunday and live unchanged on Monday.

The pattern is always the same: the vocabulary of heaven covering the architecture of self.

---

7. The Lamb Pattern: God's Consistent Remedy

Across every era of the mockery trace, God's response follows a consistent pattern: not destruction, but redemption through sacrifice.

In Eden, after the fall, God does not annihilate humanity. He provides animal skins—the first sacrifice—to cover their shame. Blood is shed. Something dies so that the image-bearers can continue.

After the golden calf, Moses intercedes: *"If You will not forgive them, blot me out of Your book"* (Exodus 32:32). A mediator stands in the gap. The pattern of substitution deepens.

The prophets, even as they confront, always end with restoration language. Isaiah thunders judgment but also whispers: *"Comfort, comfort My people"* (Isaiah 40:1). Hosea marries an unfaithful woman to demonstrate God's relentless love for a people who cannot stop mocking His covenant.

Jesus—the final answer to every era of mockery—does not come with a sword. He comes as a Lamb. The One who has every right to judge instead absorbs the judgment. The One who is mocked does not mock back. He prays: *"Father, forgive them, for they do not know what they do"* (Luke 23:34).

The mockery trace runs through every generation. But so does the Lamb pattern. And the Lamb always outlasts the mockers.

This means the answer to mockery in the church is not merely confrontation. It is the recovery of the Lamb's character—humility, sacrifice, intercession, and a refusal to retaliate. The Bride who interrupts the mockery trace does not do it by becoming harsh. She does it by becoming honest, tender, and courageous enough to absorb the cost of truth-telling.

8. What the Seven Churches Reveal

In Revelation 2–3, Jesus walks among the lampstands—the churches—and conducts a diagnostic of their spiritual condition. His letters to the seven churches are not random. They are a comprehensive map of every form the mockery trace takes within God's own people:

Ephesus had the right theology but had lost first love. The vocabulary was perfect; the heart had drifted. That is mockery through doctrinal correctness without relational devotion.

Pergamum held fast to Jesus' name but tolerated false teaching. They had courage in one area and compromise in another. Mockery through selective obedience.

Thyatira had love, service, faith, and growing works—but tolerated a Jezebel influence. Prophetic-sounding seduction into immorality and idolatry was allowed to operate because the leadership valued tolerance over holiness. Mockery through spiritual permissiveness.

Sardis had a reputation for being alive but was actually dead. The brand was strong; the substance was hollow. This is perhaps the most modern form of mockery—a church or leader whose public image has completely outpaced their private reality.

Laodicea said, *"I am rich, I have prospered, and I need nothing,"* without knowing they were *"wretched, pitiable, poor, blind, and naked"* (Revelation 3:17). Self-satisfaction that mistakes comfort for faithfulness. The most dangerous form of mockery—because the one doing it genuinely does not see it.

Each letter follows the same pattern: *"I know your works."* Jesus sees. He always sees. And His remedy is always the same: **repent and return.**

The mockery trace is persistent. But so is His mercy. The invitation to the overcomer at the end of every letter proves that God's confrontation is not a death sentence. It is a rescue mission.

The Practical Test for Your Own Organization

How do you know if the mockery trace is operating in your organization, your church, or your home? Here are five diagnostic questions:

1. **Is truth welcomed or managed?** When someone brings an honest concern, is it heard—or is it absorbed, reframed, and buried under spiritual language?

2. **Does the public story match the private reality?** If an outsider could see both your Sunday presentation and your Monday operations, would they recognize the same organization?

3. **Are questions treated as growth or as threats?** In a healthy culture, questions sharpen. In a mockery-trace culture, questions are labeled rebellion, immaturity, or lack of faith.

4. **Is spiritual language ever used to avoid accountability?** Phrases like "God told me," "this is a faith decision," or "we just need to trust" can be genuine expressions of faith—or they can be override codes that shut down honest evaluation.

5. **Who has left, and why?** If the people who leave your organization consistently cite a gap between values and reality, the mockery trace may be deeper than you think.

These questions are not designed to produce paranoia. They are designed to produce honesty. The Bride who interrupts the mockery trace does so by creating an environment where truth is safer than performance.

Formation Matrix – The Mockery Trace Timeline

Era	Form of Mockery	God's Response
Eden	Reframing God's word to justify desire	Exile from the garden; promise of redemption
Sinai	Fast verbal agreement; golden calf worship	Broken tablets; intercession of Moses
Judges	Cycles of covenant lip-service and betrayal	Repeated discipline and deliverance
Prophets	Religious performance without justice or mercy	Prophetic confrontation; exile
Jesus' Day	Tithing herbs while neglecting justice and faithfulness	"Woe to you, scribes and Pharisees"
Early Church	Image management (Ananias and Sapphira)	Immediate exposure; holy fear restored
Today	Spiritual language covering self-serving leadership	The Spirit searching the churches (Rev. 2–3)

Formation Truth

The mockery trace is not about "bad people." It is about the human heart's relentless capacity to keep the vocabulary of God while editing the authority of God. Every generation faces the same test: will you let God's word shape your life, or will you shape God's word to fit your life?

The Bride must become a people where this trace is interrupted—not by perfection, but by a culture of honesty, confession, and return. The antidote to mockery is not more performance. It is trembling again at His word.

For Leaders & Owners – Reflection Box

For Leaders & Owners:

- Where does the mockery trace show up in your organization? Not in dramatic ways—in subtle ones. In the meeting where spiritual language overrides honest data. In the culture where questioning is interpreted as rebellion.
- Is there a "Denise" in your world—someone who tried to speak truth and was absorbed or marginalized? What would it look like to reopen that door?
- If the prophets walked into your board meeting, what would they confront?

---

9. The Economics of Mockery: When Systems Enshrine the Pattern

Mockery is not only a personal sin. It can become systemic—woven into the very structures of organizations, industries, and economies.

Consider how mockery operates at scale:

- **The company that prints "People First" on the wall while treating employees as expendable.** The language is impeccable. The practice is exploitative. That is institutional mockery.
- **The church that proclaims "Come as you are" while quietly enforcing conformity.** The invitation sounds like grace. The reality is performance pressure disguised as welcome.
- **The nation that inscribes "Liberty and Justice for All" while systematically denying both to certain populations.** The words

are on the courthouse. The experience of the people tells a different story.

When mockery becomes systemic, it is especially dangerous because individuals within the system may not even see it. They inherit the language and the practice simultaneously, and because the language sounds right, they assume the practice must be right too.

This is why the prophets were so fierce. They were not confronting individuals who happened to sin. They were confronting entire systems that had enshrined the pattern of verbal honor and practical rebellion. The Temple itself had become a machine of mockery—God's own house, designed for His glory, had become what Jesus called *"a den of robbers"* (Matthew 21:13).

When Jesus drove the money changers out of the Temple, He was not having a bad day. He was performing a prophetic act that said: *This system—operating in My Father's name, using My Father's house, speaking My Father's words—has become a structure of mockery. And it ends today.*

The Bride must learn to see mockery not only in her own heart but in the systems she participates in. This requires courage, because naming systemic mockery often costs more than naming personal sin. Personal sin, you can confess quietly. Systemic mockery, you must confront publicly. And the system will push back.

But the Bride who is prepared to reign must be prepared to speak. The alternative is complicity—and complicity with a mockery system is its own form of mockery.

10. The Restoration Path: From Mockery to Trembling

If the mockery trace has run through every era, so has the restoration pattern. And the restoration always begins in the same place: trembling at God's word.

After the exile, when the remnant returned to Jerusalem, Ezra gathered the people and read the Law publicly. When they heard it, the people wept. They realized how far they had drifted. And the text says that those who *"trembled at the word of God"* (Ezra 9:4) were the ones who led the restoration.

Isaiah records God's own declaration: *"This is the one I esteem: he who is humble and contrite in spirit, and trembles at my word"* (Isaiah 66:2).

Trembling is not fear of punishment. It is the recognition that God's word is alive, present, and authoritative—and that when it speaks, the appropriate response is not commentary but compliance. Not debate but obedience. Not reinterpretation but surrender.

The modern church has largely lost this tremble. We have become commentators on God's word rather than submitted to it. We analyze, debate, blog, podcast, and discuss—but the word rarely pierces us anymore. We have developed theological calluses that protect us from the very sharpness that was meant to heal us.

The restoration from the mockery trace begins when we allow God's word to cut again. When we read *"God is not mocked"* and let it land—not as information, but as interrogation. When we hear *"To obey is better than sacrifice"* and let it evaluate our actual practices, not just our theological positions.

The Bride who will carry the weight of the age to come is the Bride who trembles again. Not in fear of God's anger—but in awe of His holiness, in reverence for His authority, and in the deep, settled awareness that His word is the most real thing in the universe.

11. Building the Anti-Mockery Culture

How do you build an organization, a family, or a church where the mockery trace is interrupted?

1. Normalize confession. In most organizations, confession is treated as weakness. In a Kingdom culture, confession is treated as strength. When leaders model honest confession—not performance confession designed to look humble, but real, specific, uncomfortable confession—the entire culture shifts. People stop hiding. Trust grows. The Spirit has room to move.

2. Reward truth-telling over comfort. The person who brings the uncomfortable truth should be thanked, not sidelined. Create structures where honest feedback is not just permitted but celebrated. A "Denise" in your organization should be your most valued voice, not your most managed one.

3. Separate spiritual language from decision-making pressure. There is nothing wrong with praying before a decision. There is something deeply wrong with using prayer as a mechanism to bypass honest evaluation. Teach your team the difference between *"Let's seek the Lord about this"* (genuine spiritual discernment) and *"God told me to do this"* (pressure tactic that shuts down discussion).

4. Audit regularly. Financial audits protect the books. Spiritual audits protect the soul. Schedule regular times—quarterly, annually—where you ask honest questions about the gap between your stated values and your actual practices. Invite outside voices. Listen to the people closest to the ground.

5. Keep the prophets close. Every organization needs at least one person who has permission to say what no one wants to hear. In the Old Testament, the prophets served this function for kings. In modern organizations, this might be a mentor, a coach, an elder, or a trusted advisor who fears God more than they fear your reaction.

The Bride who interrupts the mockery trace does not do it once. She does it as a way of life—building structures that resist the pattern, cultivating a culture where honesty is more valued than image, and returning again and again to the trembling posture that keeps the oil flowing.

Formation Practices

Inner Practice – Trace your own history. Ask the Holy Spirit: *Where has the mockery trace run through my own story?* Not in others—in you. Where have you used spiritual language to protect something God was confronting? Write it down. Let it be named.

Bodily Practice – Read the prophets aloud. This week, read one chapter of Amos, Isaiah, or Malachi aloud—slowly, standing up. Let the words vibrate in your body. The prophets were not polite. Let their urgency recalibrate yours.

Relational Practice – Welcome the uncomfortable voice. Invite someone who has been a "Denise" in your world to lunch or a phone call. Ask them: "What do you see that we aren't willing to talk about?" Do not defend. Listen as if God might be speaking through the person you least want to hear from.

Leadership Practice – Introduce one honest practice. Create one new norm in your team or organization this week: an anonymous feedback channel, a financial transparency report, or a standing agenda item titled "What are we not talking about?" Let the mockery trace be interrupted by structural honesty.

---

12. The Personal Inventory

Before moving on, take this personal inventory. It is not designed to condemn you. It is designed to help you locate where the mockery trace may be running through your own story.

In your speech:

- Do you say things about God in public that your private life contradicts?
- Do you use phrases like "God told me" or "I'm trusting God" when you actually mean "I don't want to be questioned"?
- Is there a gap between your prayer language and your lived priorities?

In your leadership:

- Are there decisions you have made that you know were driven by fear of loss rather than obedience to God?
- Have you ever used a spiritual framing to justify a financial, relational, or strategic choice that you knew was questionable?
- Is there someone in your circle who has tried to bring truth and been silenced, sidelined, or labeled?

In your inner life:

- Do you read Scripture as information about God, or do you let it interrogate you?
- When was the last time a verse made you uncomfortable enough to change something concrete?

- Is your spiritual life growing more honest over time, or more polished?

These are not trick questions. They are mirrors. And the Bride who wants to interrupt the mockery trace starts by looking honestly into her own reflection.

The prophets always started with the house of God before they addressed the nations. Jesus addressed the seven churches before He opened the seals. Judgment begins at the household of faith (1 Peter 4:17). And that household includes you.

If the mirror reveals a gap, do not despair. Despair is the enemy's response to exposure. God's response is different: *"Return to Me, and I will return to you"* (Malachi 3:7). The mockery trace breaks in the presence of honest return. It always has. It always will.

Selah – Pause Here

The serpent's first strategy was not to oppose God's word. It was to *reinterpret* it.

Ask yourself: *Where am I reinterpreting a clear word from God to fit what I've already decided?*

Let the Holy Spirit answer. He is kinder than the serpent, and more honest than your own heart.

Selah – Pause Again

Ananias and Sapphira were not punished for giving less. They were exposed for pretending they gave more.

Ask: *Where is the gap between what I present and what is actually true—in my giving, my leadership, my spiritual life?*

Let that question sit. The Spirit's light is not a weapon. It is surgery that saves.

The Role of Lament in Breaking the Mockery Cycle

One of the most overlooked tools for breaking the mockery trace is lament. Lament is not depression. It is not self-pity. It is the honest, raw, courageous act of bringing your grief before God without spin.

The Psalms are full of lament: *"How long, O Lord? Will You forget me forever?"* (Psalm 13:1). *"My God, my God, why have You forsaken me?"* (Psalm 22:1). These are not statements of unbelief. They are statements of brutal honesty—the kind of honesty that mockery cannot survive.

Mockery thrives in environments where people cannot be honest about pain. When a church culture says, "Just praise through it," or when a business culture says, "Don't bring your emotions to work," the mockery trace deepens—because people learn to perform wellness they do not feel.

Lament creates a crack in the performance. It says, "This hurts. This is wrong. And I am bringing this to God exactly as it is, without cleaning it up first."

When a leader learns to lament—before God, with trusted companions—the mockery trace begins to lose its grip. Because mockery feeds on the gap between what we say and what is true. And lament closes that gap violently.

The Bride who laments is the Bride who cannot be mocked—because she has already brought her worst truth into the open and found that God does not flinch.

Activation Prayer / Declaration

Father, I see the mockery trace—not just in history, but in my own heart. I confess that I have honored You with my lips while editing Your authority with my choices.

I do not want to be part of a pattern that has run from Eden to now. I want to be part of the interruption.

Teach me to tremble at Your word again—not in fear of punishment, but in awe of who You are. Let honesty replace performance in my life. Let obedience replace vocabulary.

Search the chambers of my heart the way You search the churches. Show me where the trace runs. And give me the courage to let You cut it out.

I choose the way of the prophets—truth over comfort. I choose the way of David—return over management. I choose the way of Jesus—the weightier matters over the impressive ones.

In Jesus' Name, amen.

Scripture for Meditation

- Genesis 3:1 – "Did God really say...?"
- Exodus 19:8 / 32:4 – Agreement and betrayal at Sinai
- Isaiah 29:13 – "This people honors Me with their lips..."
- Amos 5:21-24 – "Let justice run down like water"
- Matthew 23:23 – Tithing herbs, neglecting justice
- Acts 5:1-11 – Ananias and Sapphira: image vs. reality

Challenge – Before You Step Into the Next Chapter

Choose one area of your life where you know there is a gap between what you present and what is true. Take one concrete step to close that gap before you read another chapter. Not a perfect step—an honest one.

The next chapter confronts what happens when we stand before a holy God and realize that His mirror shows us differently than our own.

EIGHT

HOLY FEAR AND THE MIRROR: STANDING BEFORE A HOLY GOD

There is a moment in every believer's journey when the comfortable distance between them and God collapses—and they realize they are not just learning *about* Him. They are standing *before* Him. That moment is terrifying. And it is the most important moment of your formation.

Holy fear is not dread. It is not the fear of punishment. It is the sudden, overwhelming awareness that the God you have been discussing is actually *present*—and He sees everything. Not your résumé. Not your reputation. Everything.

Story Window – The Worship Leader Who Stopped Singing

Kayla led worship at a church of three thousand. Her voice could move rooms. Her Instagram had a following. Her team respected her, and invitations to lead at conferences came regularly.

One Tuesday night during rehearsal, the team was running through a set. Midway through a song about surrender, Kayla stopped. Not because of a technical problem. Not because of a wrong note.

She stopped because she heard the words she was singing: *"I surrender all."*

For the first time in years, she actually listened to what was coming out of her mouth. And something inside her said, quietly but clearly: *You don't mean that.*

The band trailed off. Someone asked if she was okay. She nodded and restarted the song. But inside, something had cracked open.

That night, alone in her car, she wept—not from shame, but from exposure. She realized that for months, perhaps years, she had been singing words of total surrender while holding back entire rooms of her life. Her relationship with money. A secret resentment toward her pastor. A habit she had excused because "nobody's perfect." A quiet pride in being the one the crowd responded to.

She had been standing in the holiest part of the service—leading others into the presence of God—while quietly withholding her own presence from Him.

The next Sunday, she didn't lead from the stage. She sat in the congregation. She didn't perform surrender. She practiced it—silently, tearfully, in a back row where no one was watching.

Over the following weeks, she met with a counselor and a trusted mentor. She named the things she had been hiding behind her gift. She made confessions she had postponed for years. The process was slow and unglamorous.

When she returned to the stage a month later, something had changed. The skill was the same. But the weight was different. People didn't just enjoy the music. They encountered something. The room shifted differently—not because her voice improved, but because her surrender was no longer a lyric. It was a posture.

What This Shows Us

You can be the most talented person in the room and still be hiding from God behind your gift. Holy fear is what happens when you stop performing for an audience and realize the Audience of One actually sees. The mirror of holiness does not show you what you project. It shows you what you carry. And that confrontation—terrifying as it is—is the doorway to genuine authority.

Scripture Deep Dive

1. Isaiah's Vision: Undone Before the Throne

Isaiah was already a prophet when he saw the Lord "high and lifted up" in chapter 6. He was not a beginner. He was a man of God. And yet his response to seeing God as He actually is was not confidence. It was collapse:

"Woe is me! For I am undone; I am a man of unclean lips, and I dwell in the midst of a people of unclean lips, for my eyes have seen the King, the Lord of hosts!" (Isaiah 6:5).

Notice what exposure produced: not self-improvement, but raw confession. Isaiah did not clean himself up before approaching. He was *undone*—and from that undoing, God sent a coal to cleanse him, and then a commission: *"Whom shall I send?"*

Holy fear does not disqualify you. It qualifies you—because it destroys the illusion that you were ever qualified on your own.

2. Moses at the Bush: Remove Your Sandals

When God appears to Moses, the first instruction is not a mission statement. It is a posture command: *"Remove your sandals, for the place where you are standing is holy ground"* (Exodus 3:5).

Before God gives Moses an assignment, He establishes awareness. You are in My presence. Take off the thing that separates your skin from this soil. Let the holiness of this moment touch you directly.

Many leaders want the commissioning without the confrontation. They want the burning bush but not the bare feet. Holy fear restores the order: *encounter first, assignment second.* God shapes who you are before He tells you what to do.

3. Peter on the Boat: Depart From Me

When Peter witnesses the miraculous catch of fish, his response is not celebration. It is terror: *"Depart from me, Lord, for I am a sinful man!"* (Luke 5:8).

Jesus does not depart. He says, *"Do not be afraid; from now on you will be catching men."*

Peter's fear was not the end of the story—it was the beginning of the call. But the call only came after the fear. There is a door you must pass through to receive real authority, and that door is the honest awareness that you are not worthy of what He is about to entrust to you.

4. John in Revelation: Falling as Dead

John—the disciple who leaned on Jesus' chest at supper—falls "as though dead" when he encounters the risen, glorified Christ in Revelation 1. The familiarity of friendship did not exempt him from the weight of glory.

Jesus' response: *"Do not be afraid. I am the First and the Last"* (Revelation 1:17).

Every major commission in Scripture passes through this pattern: **encounter → collapse → restoration → assignment.** You cannot skip the collapse and expect the assignment to carry weight. Holy fear is not a phase you graduate from. It is the atmosphere the anointing breathes in.

5. Hebrews 12: The Unshakeable Kingdom

The writer of Hebrews pulls the threads together: *"Therefore, since we are receiving a kingdom which cannot be shaken, let us have grace, by which we may serve God acceptably with reverence and godly fear. For our God is a consuming fire"* (Hebrews 12:28-29).

The unshakeable kingdom is received with reverence and awe—not with casual familiarity. The same God who calls you "friend" and "child" is a consuming fire. Friendship without reverence becomes presumption. Reverence without friendship becomes religion. The Bride carries both.

Formation Matrix – Encounters with Holiness

Person	Encounter	Response	What God Did Next
Isaiah	Saw the Lord high and lifted up	"Woe is me, I am undone"	Cleansed his lips; commissioned him
Moses	Burning bush	Hid his face in fear	Gave him the Exodus assignment
Peter	Miraculous catch of fish	"Depart from me, Lord"	Called him to fish for men

Person	Encounter	Response	What God Did Next
John	Glorified Christ in Revelation	Fell as though dead	"Do not be afraid"—then 22 chapters of revelation
Paul	Light on the Damascus road	Blinded, fell to the ground	Three days of darkness, then apostleship

---

Formation Truth

Holy fear is not the enemy of intimacy. It is intimacy's guardian. Without it, we reduce God to a concept we manage. With it, we remain in the posture where real encounter happens.

The Bride is not being formed to be comfortable in God's presence. She is being formed to be *faithful* in it—undone enough to be honest, reverent enough to be trusted, and loved enough to keep coming back.

---

6. The Proverbs Foundation: Fear of the Lord as Wisdom's Beginning

The connection between holy fear and wisdom is not incidental—it is foundational. Proverbs 9:10 declares: *"The fear of the Lord is the beginning of wisdom, and the knowledge of the Holy One is understanding."*

This means that every form of true wisdom—in leadership, in relationships, in business, in parenting—starts with holy fear. Not with strategy. Not with education. Not with experience. With the awareness that God is holy, He is present, and His ways are higher than ours.

A leader who makes decisions without holy fear will eventually trust their own intellect over God's instruction. A parent who governs without holy fear will default to control rather than formation. A church that operates without holy fear will drift into performance rather than presence.

The Bride is not merely being trained in theology. She is being trained in wisdom. And wisdom begins where holy fear begins—at the feet of a God who is both loving and terrifying, both intimate and sovereign, both Father and consuming fire.

7. Holy Fear in the Marketplace

For leaders and business owners, holy fear is not an abstract spiritual concept—it is the single most practical reality you carry into every decision.

Holy fear in the marketplace looks like:

- **Making the ethical choice even when no one is watching.** Not because of compliance, but because the One who sees in secret is evaluating your integrity.
- **Refusing to exploit people for profit.** Not because exploitation is bad PR, but because every employee, customer, and vendor is made in God's image and will be accounted for.
- **Telling the truth in financial reports.** Not because auditors might catch you, but because the God who weighed Belshazzar's kingdom on a scale weighs yours too.
- **Leading with humility rather than domination.** Not because servant leadership is trendy, but because the King you serve washed His disciples' feet.

The marketplace is not a secular space where spiritual realities don't apply. It is a jurisdiction where the Ecclesia governs—and governance under a holy King requires holy fear.

When holy fear governs your leadership, something changes in the atmosphere of your organization. People sense that there is a standard higher than the bottom line. They feel that integrity is not a policy—it is a presence. They may not be able to name it, but they know: *something is different here.*

That "something" is the fear of the Lord operating through a leader who has stood before the mirror and chosen honesty over image.

8. The Restoration Pattern: From Undone to Commissioned

Every encounter with holiness in Scripture follows the same arc:

1. **Encounter** – God reveals Himself as He truly is.
2. **Collapse** – The human response is undoing, fear, or confession.
3. **Cleansing** – God provides what the person cannot provide for themselves.
4. **Commission** – The person is sent out with a new mandate and fresh authority.

Isaiah was cleansed with a coal and sent to speak. Moses was commissioned from the bush to deliver Israel. Peter was told *"Do not be afraid"* and called to fish for men. Paul was blinded, then given sight and apostleship.

The Bride must understand that the collapse is not the end—it is the doorway. If you resist the undoing, you never receive the commissioning. If you try to maintain your composure before a holy God, you may keep your dignity, but you will lose the fresh fire.

The most dangerous leaders in the church are those who have never been undone—or who were undone once but rebuilt their walls of self-protection. The most powerful leaders are those who have learned to return regularly to the place of trembling, to let God's holiness do its work, and to receive the cleansing and commission that follow.

9. Building a Culture of Holy Fear

Holy fear is not only an individual practice—it can be cultivated in a community.

A family that practices holy fear creates an atmosphere where confession is normal, where honesty is celebrated, and where the presence of God is more valued than the performance of the members.

A church that practices holy fear creates a culture where the Word of God is not edited for comfort, where sin is confronted with love, where leaders are accountable, and where the manifest presence of God is pursued more than programs.

A business that practices holy fear creates an organization where integrity is non-negotiable, where people are treated with dignity regardless of their productivity, where the truth is told even when it's costly, and where the leader regularly acknowledges: *"We are stewards, not owners. And the Owner sees everything."*

This is what the Bride is being formed into—not a performance-driven organization with spiritual branding, but a reverent, honest, trembling-before-God community that carries His presence because it has learned to stand in His holiness.

For Leaders & Owners – Reflection Box

For Leaders & Owners:

- When was the last time you felt genuinely undone before the Lord—not in a worship service designed to produce that feeling, but in the quiet, alone, where no one was watching?
- Has your leadership become so professional that there is no room left for holy trembling?
- What would change in your decision-making if every boardroom conversation began with the awareness: *"God is actually in this room, and He sees what we're about to do"?*

---

10. The Bride's Mirror: Revelation 2–3 as a Holy-Fear Diagnostic

The letters to the seven churches in Revelation 2–3 are, in essence, God holding up a mirror to His own people. Jesus walks among the lampstands with eyes like fire—and He sees what the churches cannot see about themselves.

Each letter follows the pattern of holy-fear encounter:

"I know your works" – He sees everything. Not the curated version. Not the social media feed. The actual works.

The commendation – He affirms what is genuinely good. Holy fear does not erase encouragement. It grounds it in truth.

The confrontation – He names what needs to change. Not in generalities—in specifics. Lost love. Tolerated sin. Dead reputation. Lukewarm satisfaction.

The call to repent – The remedy is always the same: return. Not improve—return. Not rebrand—repent.

The promise to the overcomer – Every confrontation ends with hope. The one who hears and responds receives something extraordinary.

For the modern Bride, these letters are not ancient history. They are a standing invitation to stand before the mirror of holiness and let Jesus diagnose the true condition of our hearts.

Ask yourself: *If Jesus wrote a letter to my life—to my family, my business, my church—what would He commend? What would He confront? And what promise would He extend to me if I responded?*

That exercise is not hypothetical. He is writing that letter right now. The question is whether you are reading it.

11. From Trembling to Trust: The Paradox of Holy Fear

Here is the paradox that the Bride must hold: holy fear does not drive you away from God. It draws you closer.

The people in Scripture who trembled most were also the people who knew God most intimately. Abraham was called "friend of God"—and fell on his face before Him. Moses spoke with God "face to face, as a man speaks to a friend"—and asked to see His glory, only to be hidden in the cleft of a rock because the fullness would have killed him. David danced before the ark in wild abandon—and then trembled when a man was struck dead for touching it.

Intimacy and awe are not opposites. They are two sides of the same coin. You cannot know God deeply without trembling. And you cannot tremble rightly without knowing His love.

The modern church has often separated these. We have created one stream that emphasizes intimacy—*"Come as you are, God loves you, He's your friend"*—and another stream that emphasizes holiness—*"God is holy, sin has consequences, fear the Lord."* But the Bride needs both streams flowing through her simultaneously.

When you only have intimacy without awe, you become casual. Prayer becomes chatty. Sin becomes "a struggle" that never quite gets resolved. You lose the weight that made your faith formidable.

When you only have awe without intimacy, you become rigid. Prayer becomes performance. Holiness becomes legalism. You lose the tenderness that made your faith beautiful.

The Bride who is being formed for the age to come carries both: the intimacy of a beloved who knows she is cherished, and the reverence of a servant who knows she serves a consuming fire. She does not choose one over the other. She holds both—and in the tension, she becomes the most fully alive, most deeply grounded, most powerfully anointed expression of the Church the world has ever seen.

12. The Mirror in Your Monday

Holy fear is not a Sunday experience. It is a Monday practice.

Every decision you make is a mirror moment. Every email you send, every conversation you have, every transaction you complete—these are all opportunities to stand before a holy God and choose: *Will I honor You here, or will I manage the situation on my own terms?*

This is not about perfection. It is about awareness. The person who lives in holy fear does not live in anxiety. They live in attentiveness. They carry a quiet, constant awareness that God is present—in the office, in the car, in the difficult conversation, in the financial decision.

That awareness changes everything:

- You don't cut corners when no one is watching—because Someone always is.
- You don't exploit people for advantage—because they belong to Someone who sees.
- You don't spin the truth to protect your image—because the One who matters most already knows the truth.
- You don't coast on yesterday's anointing—because today's decisions are being weighed on today's scales.

The Bride who carries holy fear into Monday morning is the Bride who carries authority. Because authority is not given to the talented. It is given to the trustworthy. And trustworthiness is formed in the daily, unglamorous practice of living as if a holy God is actually watching—because He is.

Formation Practices

Inner Practice – The five-minute mirror. Set a timer for five minutes. Sit in silence with this one sentence: *Lord, show me what You see.* Do not lead the conversation. Do not bring an agenda. Let the Holy Spirit hold up His mirror. Whatever He shows you, write it down without editing.

Bodily Practice – Kneel when you pray this week. For one full week, begin your prayer time on your knees. Not because kneeling earns something—but because posture teaches the heart. Let your body remember that you are approaching a holy God, not managing a spiritual routine.

Relational Practice – Confess something real to someone safe. Holy fear produces confession, not isolation. Find one trusted person and share one thing the Spirit has shown you in the mirror this week. Not a vague generality—something specific. Let their witness hold you accountable to what God has revealed.

Leadership Practice – Begin one meeting differently. Choose one leadership meeting this week and begin it with two minutes of silence—no agenda, no opening prayer formula—just stillness before a holy God. Then ask the room: "Is there anything we need to be honest about before we proceed?"

---

13. A Theology of Trembling

The modern church has developed a sophisticated theology of grace, a robust theology of love, and an extensive theology of identity. What it has largely lost is a theology of trembling.

Trembling in Scripture is not a sign of immaturity. It is a sign of encounter. The most mature people in the Bible trembled the most—because they saw God the most clearly.

Consider the progression:

- **Abraham fell on his face** when God appeared to him to confirm the covenant (Genesis 17:3).
- **The nation of Israel trembled** at the base of Sinai when God descended in fire and thunder (Exodus 19:16).
- **David trembled** when Uzzah was struck dead for touching the ark—and learned that God's presence must be carried God's way (2 Samuel 6:9).
- **Habakkuk's body trembled** when God revealed what was coming, and yet he declared: *"Though the fig tree does not blossom... yet I will rejoice in the Lord"* (Habakkuk 3:16-18).
- **The women at the tomb trembled** when they encountered the angel announcing the resurrection—and then ran with joy to tell the disciples (Mark 16:8).

Trembling is not the opposite of faith. It is the evidence that you have encountered something real. A faith that never trembles may be a faith that has never truly encountered the living God.

The Bride needs this theology restored—not to make people afraid, but to make them reverent. Reverence creates capacity. A reverential heart can receive more of God than a casual one, because it approaches Him with the seriousness that His glory deserves.

When you restore trembling to your spiritual life, something remarkable happens: your prayers gain weight. Your worship deepens. Your obedience becomes less about obligation and more about awe. You stop trying to use God for your purposes and start letting Him use you for His.

That is the atmosphere where the anointing thrives. That is the environment the oil requires. That is the posture of the Bride who will carry the weight of the age to come.

Selah – Pause Here

Isaiah was already a prophet when he was undone. He was not a beginner. He was experienced, respected, anointed.

Ask yourself: *Has my experience with God made me more reverent—or more familiar?*

There is a difference between confidence in His grace and casualness with His presence. Let the Spirit recalibrate.

Selah – Pause Again

Peter said, *"Depart from me."* Jesus said, *"Follow Me."*

The door to your deepest calling may be standing on the other side of your most honest confession. Do not run from the mirror. Walk toward it. What you find there is not condemnation—it is the beginning of a deeper trust.

---

14. The Physical Dimension of Holy Fear

Scripture repeatedly shows that encounters with holiness affect the body:

- Moses' face shone after being in God's presence—so brightly that he had to wear a veil.
- Daniel lost all strength when confronted by an angelic being: *"No strength remained in me... I retained no strength"* (Daniel 10:8).
- The soldiers guarding Jesus' tomb became like dead men when the angel appeared (Matthew 28:4).
- Paul was physically blinded on the Damascus road.

Holy fear is not merely a mental or emotional experience. It registers in the body. Trembling, weeping, falling, loss of strength—these are physical responses to spiritual reality.

This matters because the modern church has become almost entirely cerebral in its approach to God. We process theology intellectually. We evaluate worship aesthetically. We make spiritual decisions rationally. And while none of these things are wrong, they can become shields that prevent the body from experiencing what the spirit is encountering.

When you practice kneeling, fasting, raising your hands, lying prostrate, or simply sitting in silence until your body stills—you are creating space for holy fear to register at a level deeper than thought. Your nervous system, your muscles, your posture—all of these can be trained to respond to God's presence.

A leader whose body has learned to tremble before God carries a different authority than a leader whose body has only learned to perform on stage. The first carries weight. The second carries presence. They are not the same thing.

15. Teaching Your Children Holy Fear

If you are a parent, one of the greatest gifts you can give your children is the experience of holy fear—not through harsh discipline or fear-based religion, but through your own genuine reverence.

Children are remarkably perceptive. They can tell the difference between a parent who performs spirituality and a parent who is genuinely moved by God's presence. When your child sees you weep in worship—not for effect, but because something real is happening—they are learning holy fear.

When your child hears you confess a real mistake, not as a lesson for their benefit but as an honest response to God's conviction—they are learning holy fear.

When your child observes that you make a business decision that costs you money because "it's what God would want"—they are learning holy fear.

You do not teach holy fear by lecturing about it. You teach it by living it—by letting your children see that there is a God who is real, who is present, and who is more important to you than your image, your comfort, or your success.

That is the inheritance the Bride passes to the next generation: not theology about holiness, but the lived experience of trembling before a God who is both terrifying and beautiful.

Activation Prayer / Declaration

Father, I come to You—not with performance, but with trembling.

I have grown too familiar. I have approached You casually when I should have approached You in awe. I have treated Your presence like a routine instead of a holy encounter.

Undo me, Lord. Show me what You see. Let Your holiness touch the places I have been protecting.

Like Isaiah, I confess: I am a person of unclean lips, living among a people of unclean lips. But I trust that the coal from Your altar can cleanse what my effort cannot fix.

Like Moses, I take off my sandals. I acknowledge that the ground of my life is holy—not because of me, but because You are present in it.

Like Peter, I fall before You—not to be sent away, but to be called deeper.

Restore holy fear in my life. Not the fear of punishment—but the awe that guards my intimacy with You, the reverence that protects the oil, and the trembling that makes me trustworthy.

In Jesus' Name, amen.

Scripture for Meditation

- Isaiah 6:1-8 – "Woe is me, I am undone"
- Exodus 3:1-6 – "Remove your sandals; this is holy ground"
- Luke 5:8 – "Depart from me, Lord, for I am a sinful man"

- Revelation 1:12-18 – John falls as though dead before the risen Christ
- Hebrews 12:28-29 – "Our God is a consuming fire"
- Proverbs 9:10 – "The fear of the Lord is the beginning of wisdom"

Challenge – Before You Step Into the Next Chapter

Before you turn this page, do something you may not have done in a long time: kneel. Not symbolically—physically. Put your knees on the floor and say: *Lord, I am Yours. Search me. Show me what the mirror reveals. And give me the courage to respond.*

Let that posture carry you into the next chapter, where we will explore the Ecclesia—the called-out ones who are born from Zion and carry the King's authority into the earth.

NINE

ECCLESIA: CALLED-OUT ONES, BORN FROM ZION

The word *church* has been domesticated. It conjures images of buildings, programs, Sunday services, and volunteer sign-up sheets. But the word Jesus actually used—*Ecclesia*—had nothing to do with any of that. It was a political word. A governing word. A word that described a legislative assembly called out to make binding decisions on behalf of a city or region.

When Jesus said, *"I will build My Ecclesia, and the gates of hell shall not prevail against it"* (Matthew 16:18), He was not announcing a worship service. He was announcing a governing body.

This chapter reclaims that word—and with it, your identity.

Story Window – The City That Changed from the Inside

Carmen was a public school principal in a struggling district. Test scores were low, teacher retention was worse, and the community had largely given up hope. Most principals before her had lasted two years. She was in year seven.

What no one outside her closest circle knew was that Carmen operated from a conviction most educators would find irrelevant: she believed she was placed in that school by God, not by the district office. She did not preach. She did not put Bible verses on the walls. But she led with a Psalm 82 awareness—*"How long will you judge unjustly and show partiality to the wicked? Defend the weak and the fatherless; uphold the cause of the poor and the oppressed."*

She restructured the counseling program around trauma-informed care—not because it was trending, but because she believed every child was made in God's image and deserved to be treated accordingly. She fought for funding that others assumed was impossible. She stayed late, not to be seen, but because she believed her presence in that building was an act of governance, not just employment.

Over seven years, the school transformed. Not overnight. Not with a single breakthrough. With steady, faithful, daily authority exercised in love.

The day a state official visited and asked, "What changed here?"—Carmen didn't mention a program or a grant. She said, "We decided these kids were worth fighting for."

That is Ecclesia in action.

What This Shows Us

Ecclesia is not limited to a church building. It operates wherever the called-out ones carry the King's authority into the structures of the world. Carmen did not govern with religious language. She governed with kingdom values—justice, dignity, persistence, and sacrificial presence. The gates of hell did not prevail against that school because someone was functioning as Ecclesia inside it.

Scripture Deep Dive

1. The Word Jesus Chose

In Matthew 16:18, Jesus could have used many Greek words. He could have said *synagoge* (assembly). He could have said *koinonia* (fellowship). He could have said *laos* (people). He chose *Ecclesia.*

In the Greek-speaking world of the first century, an *ecclesia* was:

- A formal assembly of citizens called out of the general population.
- A governing body with legal authority to make decisions for the city.
- A legislative group that set policy, resolved disputes, and represented the governing power.

When Jesus said, "I will build My Ecclesia," He was not saying, "I will start a club." He was saying: **I am forming a governing assembly that carries My authority on the earth.**

2. The Gates of Hell: Defensive, Not Offensive

Notice the architecture of Jesus' promise: *"The gates of hell shall not prevail against it."*

Gates are defensive structures. Gates do not chase you. They hold territory. Jesus is not describing a church hiding behind walls hoping hell doesn't break in. He is describing an advancing assembly that storms the gates of darkness—and those gates cannot hold.

This reframes the Bride's identity entirely. She is not a victim trying to survive until rescue. She is a governing body advancing the King's rule into occupied territory.

3. The Keys of the Kingdom

Immediately after the Ecclesia declaration, Jesus says: *"I will give you the keys of the kingdom of heaven; whatever you bind on earth will be bound in heaven, and whatever you loose on earth will be loosed in heaven"* (Matthew 16:19).

Keys represent:

- **Access** – the authority to open doors no one else can open.
- **Administration** – the right to manage the King's household.
- **Jurisdiction** – the legal standing to bind and loose.

The Ecclesia does not merely pray and hope for the best. It administrates heaven's decisions on the earth. Binding and loosing are courtroom language—legal rulings made by those authorized to make them.

4. Born from Zion, Not from Denomination

Psalm 87 declares: *"Of Zion it will be said, 'This one and that one were born in her'"* (Psalm 87:5). The Ecclesia's origin is not a denomination, tradition, or movement. It is Zion—the mountain of God's presence.

This matters because it means:

- Your authority comes from heaven, not from a board vote.
- Your identity is in the King, not in an institution.
- Your citizenship is in the city of God, even while you serve in the cities of men.

When you understand yourself as born from Zion, you stop waiting for permission from earthly structures to exercise heavenly authority. You carry an identity that precedes and outlasts every organization you belong to.

5. Psalm 82: Governing Among the Rulers

In Psalm 82, God stands in the assembly of the gods—the spiritual rulers and powers—and confronts their failure: *"How long will you judge unjustly? Defend the poor and fatherless; do justice to the afflicted and needy"* (Psalm 82:2-3).

This psalm reveals that governance in the heavenly places involves justice on the earth. The Ecclesia inherits this mandate: to stand in the spiritual assembly and execute righteous judgment—not with swords, but with prayer, intercession, declaration, and lived-out justice.

6. Acts 19: The Ecclesia Confronts a City's Economy

In Ephesus, Paul's preaching caused such upheaval that the entire city's economy—built on idolatry and the worship of Artemis—was threatened. The silversmiths who made idols started a riot. And the word Luke uses to describe the city gathering that resulted? *Ecclesia.*

The same word Jesus used for His people was the same word used for the city's governing assembly. Luke is making a point: there are two ecclesias in Ephesus—the city's and the King's. And they are in direct conflict.

This is the Bride's reality. She is not a subculture hiding inside a larger society. She is an alternative governing authority—the King's assembly in the midst of the city's assembly. And where she carries His values faithfully, the gates of hell cannot hold.

Formation Matrix – Ecclesia vs. "Church" as Commonly Understood

Dimension	Common "Church" Mindset	Ecclesia Identity
Purpose	Worship services and programs	Governing assembly carrying the King's authority
Posture	Defensive – hoping to survive	Advancing – gates of hell cannot prevail
Authority	Delegated by a denomination or leader	Delegated by the King Himself
Scope	Sunday gathering	Every sphere: education, business, government, family
Identity source	Membership in an organization	Born from Zion; citizenship in heaven
Tool of influence	Events and outreach	Binding, loosing, justice, intercession, presence

---

Formation Truth

You are not just "going to church." You *are* the Ecclesia. You carry keys. You have jurisdiction. You were born from Zion. And the gates of every system built on injustice, idolatry, and deception cannot stand against the assembly Jesus is building.

This identity does not make you aggressive or arrogant. It makes you responsible. You cannot claim Ecclesia authority on Sunday and abandon Ecclesia responsibility on Monday.

---

7. The Ecclesia and the Kingdom of God

There is a critical distinction that must be understood: the Ecclesia is not the Kingdom, but it is the primary agent of the Kingdom on the earth.

The Kingdom of God is God's reign—His sovereign rule over all creation. It existed before the church and will exist after every earthly institution has passed away. But in this present age, the Ecclesia has been given the keys to administrate that Kingdom in the earth.

Think of it this way: a kingdom has a king, a territory, laws, and citizens. The King is Jesus. The territory is "all authority in heaven and on earth" (Matthew 28:18). The laws are the principles of the Kingdom revealed in Scripture. And the citizens are the Ecclesia—the called-out assembly authorized to enforce the King's decrees.

This means the Ecclesia is not a club, a social group, or a religious organization. It is a **governing embassy of heaven operating on foreign soil.** An embassy carries the laws and authority of the home country, even while located in a different nation. When you walk into an American embassy in a foreign city, you are technically standing on American soil. The laws of the host country do not supersede the authority of the home nation within that space.

The Ecclesia functions the same way. Wherever the called-out ones gather—in a home, a boardroom, a school, a neighborhood—they carry the authority of heaven. The "laws" of darkness do not supersede the King's authority within that jurisdiction.

This is why prayer is not begging. Prayer is the Ecclesia exercising its legal right to invoke the King's authority over situations that fall within its jurisdiction. When you pray *"Your Kingdom come, Your will be done on earth as it is in heaven,"* you are not making a wish. You are issuing a governmental decree.

8. The Ecclesia in the Public Square

The early church did not confine its activity to private gatherings. The Ecclesia confronted public systems.

In Acts 16, Paul and Silas are imprisoned for disrupting the economy of fortune-telling in Philippi. They don't quietly submit—they worship, the earth shakes, the jailer is saved, and then Paul insists on a public vindication from the magistrates. Why? Because the Ecclesia's authority is not private. It operates in the public sphere.

In Acts 17, Paul stands in the Areopagus—the intellectual governing assembly of Athens—and declares the resurrection. He does not water down his message for the audience. He confronts their altar to an unknown god with the revelation of the God who made everything.

In Acts 19, the entire economy of Ephesus is disrupted because Paul's preaching has turned people away from idol worship. The silversmiths riot—not because Paul was wrong, but because the Ecclesia's message was threatening the economic infrastructure built on idolatry.

The pattern is consistent: the Ecclesia does not hide in private spirituality. It enters the public arena—economic systems, intellectual debates, political structures—and declares the King's authority. Not with violence. Not with manipulation. But with truth, power, and an unwillingness to bow to any authority that sets itself against the knowledge of God.

9. Your Workplace as an Ecclesia Outpost

If you are a business owner, a manager, a teacher, a healthcare worker, or any kind of leader—your sphere of influence is not separate from your Ecclesia identity. It is an expression of it.

When you hire with integrity, you are exercising Ecclesia authority over economic systems. When you create a culture where people are valued and truth is told, you are advancing the Kingdom in that space. When you refuse to participate in exploitative practices—even when it costs you market share—you are governing as one who carries the keys of the Kingdom.

Carmen's school was an Ecclesia outpost. She did not hang Scripture on the walls or hold chapel services. But she carried the King's values—justice, dignity, sacrificial presence—into a broken system and watched it transform over seven years.

You do not need to turn your workplace into a church to function as Ecclesia. You need to carry the King's heart, the King's standards, and the King's authority into every room you enter. That is what it means to be called out—not called out *of* the world, but called out *from* conformity to the world's patterns and called *into* governing with heaven's authority.

The gates of hell in your industry—exploitation, dishonesty, dehumanization, greed—cannot stand against a man or woman who walks into work every morning knowing: *I am Ecclesia. I carry keys. And the King has given me jurisdiction here.*

For Leaders & Owners – Reflection Box

For Leaders & Owners:

- Do you see your workplace as a mission field only—or as a jurisdiction where you carry the King's authority?
- What would change if you walked into your office, your shop floor, or your boardroom with Psalm 82 awareness—knowing that you are governing in a spiritual assembly, not just running a business?
- Where are the "gates of hell" in your industry—the entrenched systems of injustice, exploitation, or deception? What would it look like for your Ecclesia identity to confront them?

---

10. The Ecclesia and Cultural Engagement

One of the greatest confusions in the modern church is the relationship between the Ecclesia and culture. Two extremes dominate:

The withdrawal model says the church should retreat from culture, build its own subculture, and wait for Jesus to return. This produces insular communities that are deeply connected to each other but increasingly disconnected from the world they were sent to serve.

The assimilation model says the church should embrace culture, adopt its language and values, and meet people where they are. This often produces communities that look indistinguishable from the surrounding society—with a thin veneer of spirituality that makes no real demands and offers no real transformation.

Neither model is Ecclesia.

The Ecclesia model is **engagement without conformity.** The called-out ones are sent into the culture—not to hide from it, not to become it, but to carry the King's authority within it.

Daniel is perhaps the best Old Testament picture of this. He was embedded in the heart of Babylonian culture—educated in its language, serving in its government, navigating its politics. Yet he never compromised his core allegiance. He prayed with his windows open. He refused the king's food. He interpreted dreams by the Spirit, not by Babylonian magic. And because of his faithfulness, he rose to the highest levels of influence—carrying God's wisdom into the decision-making chambers of a pagan empire.

Daniel did not withdraw. He did not assimilate. He governed as Ecclesia inside Babylon.

This is the model for the modern Bride. You are not called to retreat from the marketplace, the education system, the entertainment industry, the healthcare system, or the government. You are called to enter them as Daniel entered Babylon—with integrity, wisdom, courage, and an uncompromising allegiance to the King.

11. The Ecclesia's Weapon: Prayer as Governance

The primary weapon of the Ecclesia is not political power, economic leverage, or social influence. It is prayer.

But not prayer as we commonly understand it—prayer as a personal request list presented to a distant God. The Ecclesia prays as a governing body exercising its legal authority.

When the early church prayed in Acts 4, they did not pray for escape. They prayed for boldness: *"Lord, look upon their threats, and grant to Your servants that with all boldness they may speak Your word"* (Acts 4:29). And the result? *"The place where they were assembled together was shaken"* (Acts 4:31).

Their prayer shook the physical environment. That is not a metaphor. When the Ecclesia prays from its true identity—not begging, but governing; not hoping, but decreeing—something shifts in the spiritual atmosphere, and that shift manifests in the natural world.

This is what Jesus meant when He said, *"Whatever you bind on earth will be bound in heaven"* (Matthew 16:19). The Ecclesia does not make suggestions to heaven. It administrates heaven's decisions on earth.

Consider what this means practically:

- When you pray over your business, you are not asking God to please bless your plans. You are exercising your Ecclesia authority to invite the King's rule into that space—and to bind every pattern of exploitation, dishonesty, and fear that has operated there.
- When you pray over your city, you are not passively hoping things get better. You are standing in your Zion-born identity and loosing the King's justice, mercy, and truth into the systems of that city.
- When you pray over your family, you are not just a worried parent. You are the governing authority God has placed in that household, with the right to bind generational patterns and loose the inheritance of the Kingdom over your children.

Prayer is not the Ecclesia's backup plan. It is her primary mode of governance.

12. The Ecclesia and the Gates: What Are You Advancing Against?

Jesus said the gates of hell would not prevail against the Ecclesia. But what are those gates in your life?

Gates represent entrenched positions—systems, patterns, and strongholds that have held territory for generations. In your life and sphere of influence, they might look like:

- **A generational pattern of poverty or financial dysfunction** that has kept your family in bondage for decades.
- **A culture of fear in your workplace** that suppresses creativity, truth-telling, and genuine leadership.

- **A systemic injustice in your industry** that exploits vulnerable people for profit.

- **A pattern of broken relationships** that has marked your family tree for generations.

- **A spiritual stronghold over your city** that manifests as apathy, addiction, violence, or despair.

These are gates. They are defensive structures that hold occupied territory. And Jesus has declared that when the Ecclesia advances, these gates cannot hold.

But the Ecclesia must advance. Gates do not fall on their own. They fall when the governing assembly of the King—carrying His keys, standing in His authority, speaking His Word, walking in His holiness—moves toward them with deliberate, faithful, persistent pressure.

This is why the Bride cannot afford to be passive. Every day you do not advance is a day the gates remain standing. Every prayer you do not pray is a decree that goes unissued. Every act of justice you do not pursue is territory that stays occupied.

You are Ecclesia. You carry keys. The gates are waiting for you to arrive.

Formation Practices

Inner Practice – Rename yourself. This week, every morning before you start your day, say aloud: *I am part of the Ecclesia of Jesus Christ. I carry keys. I have jurisdiction. I was born from Zion.* Let this reshape how you see yourself before you interact with anyone else.

Bodily Practice – Walk your territory. Choose a physical space you are responsible for—your office, your campus, your neighborhood—and walk through it slowly, praying: *"Lord, Your kingdom come in this place. Your will be done here as it is in heaven."* Let your feet carry authority, not just your words.

Relational Practice – Identify your governing council. Ecclesia was never a solo project. Identify two or three people who share your conviction about carrying the King's authority into the world. Begin meeting regularly—not for Bible study alone, but for governing prayer: *What is God saying about* *our city? What needs to be bound? What needs to be loosed? Where are we being sent?*

Leadership Practice – Confront one gate. Identify one entrenched pattern of injustice, dishonesty, or exploitation in your sphere of influence. Take one deliberate step to confront it this week—not with anger, but with the quiet authority of someone who knows their King has already won.

---

13. The Ecclesia and Generational Thinking

One of the most damaging effects of escape theology (which we will address more fully in the next chapter) on the Ecclesia is the loss of generational thinking.

If you believe you are leaving at any moment, you do not build for the next generation. You build for survival. But the Ecclesia was never designed for one generation. It was designed to carry the King's authority across centuries.

Consider the scope of Jesus' promise: *"I will build My Ecclesia, and the gates of hell shall not prevail against it."* He did not say, "I will build My Ecclesia for your generation." He said He would build it—period. Ongoing. Multigenerational. Unstoppable across time.

This means the Ecclesia is responsible for:

- **Raising up successors.** Not just training the next wave of leaders, but transferring the identity, the authority, and the governing wisdom that the current generation carries. Victor's story from Chapter 5 is relevant here: he built something that could not outlive him because he never transferred the core of what he carried.

- **Building institutions that last.** Not bureaucracies—living institutions that carry Kingdom DNA across generations. Schools, businesses, hospitals, legal frameworks, artistic traditions, theological academies—all of these can be Ecclesia outposts if they are built with generational intentionality.

- **Preserving and transmitting wisdom.** The Psalms were Israel's hymnal—songs passed from generation to generation, carrying theological truth in memorable, singable form. The Ecclesia needs its own equivalents: writings, liturgies, practices, and stories that carry the King's truth into the future.

- **Planting seeds you may never see harvested.** The person who plants an oak tree is rarely the person who sits in its shade. Generational thinking requires the humility to invest in outcomes you will not personally enjoy. That is not futility. That is faith.

The Ecclesia that thinks generationally governs differently. It does not make decisions based solely on this quarter's results. It asks: *What will this decision produce in twenty years? In a hundred years? When my great-grandchildren inherit what I've built, what will they find?*

That is the mind of a governing assembly. That is the heart of a Bride who carries keys—not just for today, but for the generations to come.

Selah – Pause Here

Jesus said, *"I will build My Ecclesia."*

Not your denomination. Not your movement. Not your brand. *His.* And the gates of hell will not prevail against it.

Ask: *Am I participating in what Jesus is building—or am I building something else and asking Him to bless it?*

Selah – Pause Again

Carmen didn't preach in her school. She governed. She exercised authority through love, justice, and faithful presence—for seven years.

Ask: *Where has God placed me as Ecclesia—not to preach, but to govern? Am I showing up with the weight of that identity, or treating it as just a job?*

---

14. The Ecclesia and Justice

The Ecclesia cannot claim to carry the King's authority while ignoring the King's primary concern. And throughout Scripture, one of God's primary concerns is justice—particularly justice for those who cannot secure it for themselves.

"Learn to do good; seek justice, correct oppression; bring justice to the fatherless, plead the widow's cause" (Isaiah 1:17).

"What does the Lord require of you but to do justice, and to love mercy, and to walk humbly with your God?" (Micah 6:8).

"Religion that is pure and undefiled before God the Father is this: to visit orphans and widows in their affliction, and to keep oneself unstained from the world" (James 1:27).

The Ecclesia that prays powerful prayers but ignores systemic injustice in its own backyard is not functioning as a governing assembly. It is functioning as a spiritual club.

Justice is not a side project of the Ecclesia. It is central to its mandate. When Jesus announced His mission in Luke 4, He quoted Isaiah: *"The Spirit of the Lord is upon Me, because He has anointed Me to proclaim good news to the poor... to proclaim liberty to the captives... to set at liberty those who are oppressed."*

The anointing and justice are inseparable. The Bride who carries the anointing but neglects justice is carrying oil in a cracked vessel—it will leak out, no matter how full she thinks she is.

For leaders and business owners, this means: your business practices are not separate from your spiritual authority. How you treat the lowest-paid employee in your organization is a direct reflection of your Ecclesia identity. How your supply chain operates, how your pricing affects vulnerable communities, how your hiring practices include or exclude—all of this is governance. And the King is watching how His governors govern.

15. The Ecclesia as Family

One final dimension must be named: the Ecclesia is not only a governing body. It is a family.

Paul calls the church *"the household of God"* (Ephesians 2:19). Jesus taught His disciples to pray *"Our Father."* The Ecclesia is not a corporation with a spiritual mission statement. It is brothers and sisters carrying the family name into the world.

This means the Ecclesia operates with:

- **Unconditional belonging.** You do not earn your place in the family. You are born into it.
- **Mutual accountability.** Family members do not ignore each other's struggles. They confront in love and restore in gentleness.
- **Shared inheritance.** The resources of the Kingdom belong to the whole family, not to the most powerful members.
- **Generational continuity.** The family extends backward and forward in time. You inherit from those who came before and invest in those who come after.

When the Ecclesia loses its family character, it becomes either a corporation (efficient but cold) or a movement (exciting but unstable). The Bride is neither. She is a household—warm, accountable, enduring, and anchored in the love of the Father who called her into being.

Activation Prayer / Declaration

Jesus, You said You would build Your Ecclesia, and the gates of hell would not prevail.

I receive that identity. I am not just attending church. I am the Church—Your governing assembly, born from Zion, carrying Your keys.

I bind every lie that says I am powerless, passive, or irrelevant in the systems of this world. I loose the authority You have delegated—to pray, to declare, to intercede, to govern, and to advance Your kingdom in every sphere I touch.

I will not retreat behind comfort. I will not hide behind humility. I will stand, as Your Ecclesia, in the places You have assigned me—my home, my workplace, my city, my generation.

Build Your Ecclesia through me. And let the gates of hell tremble.

In Jesus' Name, amen.

Scripture for Meditation

- Matthew 16:18-19 – "I will build My Ecclesia... I give you the keys"
- Psalm 87:5 – "Of Zion it will be said, 'This one was born in her'"
- Psalm 82:1-4 – "God stands in the divine assembly... Defend the poor"
- Acts 19:23-41 – The Ecclesia confronts Ephesus's idolatrous economy
- Ephesians 3:10 – The manifold wisdom of God displayed through the Ecclesia

---

Challenge – Before You Step Into the Next Chapter

Write down the one place where you know God has given you jurisdiction—a school, a business, a family, a neighborhood. Then ask Him: *What does it look like for me to govern this space as Ecclesia, not just occupy it?*

Carry that answer into the next chapter, where we will dismantle the escape theology that has convinced the Bride she was meant to flee—when in fact she was always meant to stand.

TEN

THE BRIDE WHO DOES NOT FLEE: DISMANTLING ESCAPE THEOLOGY

For generations, a significant portion of the Western church has been shaped by a single expectation: *We are leaving.* Any moment now, Jesus will pull us out of this world, and everything here will burn. That belief—sincere, widely taught, deeply felt—has quietly shaped how the Bride sees herself, how she leads, how she invests, and how she prepares for the future.

This chapter is not an attack on people who hold that view. Many of the most faithful believers you know were raised on it, comforted by it, and anchored by it during hard times. But comfort and clarity are not the same thing. And the Bride cannot afford to prepare for escape when she was designed for arrival.

Story Window – The Business Owner Who Stopped Building

Ethan ran a manufacturing company his father had started. It was solid—profitable, well-staffed, deeply embedded in the local economy. But Ethan carried a quiet belief that shaped everything he did: *It's all going to burn anyway.*

He had grown up hearing it in church: the rapture could happen at any moment. The world was getting worse. Investing in long-term projects was pointless because Jesus was coming to take the church out of here before the real trouble began.

For years, that belief didn't seem to cost anything. But as Ethan's company grew and required bigger decisions—infrastructure upgrades, succession planning, community investment—the belief started to show up in his leadership.

When his operations manager recommended a five-year investment in sustainable manufacturing, Ethan hesitated. *Five years? We might not be here in five years.* When his HR director flagged a toxic culture developing under a high-performing sales leader, Ethan shrugged it off. *Why fight that battle now? We just need to hold things together.*

His best young leader left, frustrated by the lack of vision. His community engagement dwindled. His equipment aged. His staff sensed that the owner was coasting—not because he was lazy, but because something inside him had decided the future wasn't worth building for.

Then one Sunday, a visiting teacher said something that lodged in Ethan's chest like a splinter: *"If you really believed Jesus was coming to reign here—not to evacuate you, but to dwell with you in a renewed creation—would you lead differently?"*

The question wouldn't leave him.

Over the next weeks, that quiet revelation began to rearrange him. He started thinking like someone whose work mattered to Jesus—beyond this quarter and beyond his lifetime. He invested in training a younger leadership team instead of trying to coast to retirement. He made the costly decision to upgrade outdated, polluting equipment—not because it boosted profits, but because he believed the King cared about the world he had been stewarding. He sat down with the toxic high-performer and, for the first time, led that person toward either repentance or exit, instead of hoping to avoid confrontation until the rapture.

His company did not suddenly become trial-proof. But something shifted in its atmosphere. The staff began to sense that their work was part of a story bigger than "hang on until we're gone." Younger employees started taking ownership. Clients noticed the integrity in how they handled difficulty. Even the way Ethan prayed changed—from *"Lord, get us out,"* to *"Lord, make us faithful in this."*

What This Shows Us

This is what escape theology does to a leader: it makes long-term obedience optional and long-term investment feel pointless. This is what royal-arrival theology does: it gives courage to build, to repent, to steward people and places as if Jesus really is coming *here,* and as if what you build with Him will matter when He does.

Scripture Deep Dive

1. The Loudest Passage: What 1 Thessalonians 4 Actually Describes

The escape narrative leans hardest on one passage:

"The Lord Himself will descend from heaven with a shout, with the voice of an archangel, and with the trumpet of God. The dead in Christ will rise first. Then we who are alive and remain shall be caught up together with them in the clouds to meet the Lord in the air. And thus we shall always be with the Lord" (1 Thessalonians 4:16–17).

Notice the elements: the Lord descends; a commanding shout; an archangel's voice; the trumpet of God; the dead raised; the living caught up. Nothing about this sounds secret. It is the loudest, most public event in human history.

The key hinge is the phrase *"to meet the Lord in the air."* In the ancient world, the Greek word for "meet" (*apantēsis*) was a technical term: it described a civic delegation that went out of a city to greet a visiting king and then **escorted him back in.**

Picture it: A king approaches. Citizens are summoned out to meet him. They form a procession around him. They accompany him back into the city he has come to rule.

That is the picture: the risen and transformed saints going out to greet the King as He arrives in glory, then sharing in His public return. Not a vanished Church leaving the earth behind, but a **revealed Bride welcoming the King back to His world.**

2. As in the Days of Noah: Who Actually Left?

Jesus said His coming would be *"as it was in the days of Noah."* In Noah's day, the righteous were preserved. The wicked were swept away. The earth was cleansed and renewed. Noah did not escape the planet. He passed through judgment into a renewed world.

When Jesus speaks of some being "taken" and others "left," we often assume *taken* means *rescued.* But in Noah's story, the ones *taken* by the flood were those under judgment. The one *left standing on the earth* was the righteous man and his family.

The pattern is consistent: God preserves His people. He passes through judgment with them. He brings them into a cleansed creation. That is the opposite of an evacuation mindset.

3. Sabbath and Hebrews 4: Rest as Completion, Not Exit

In Genesis, God rests on the seventh day—and the text never says "evening and morning" on that day. The rest remains open. In Hebrews 4: *"There remains, therefore, a Sabbath rest for the people of God."*

Rest is not merely a day. It is a state we are being invited into. Sabbath is about work completed, creation ordered, God dwelling with His people.

When Jesus declares *"It is finished"* at the cross and then rises, He is inaugurating new-creation Sabbath. The final appearing of Christ is not about abandoning creation. It is about completing that rest—bringing heaven's order fully into earth.

Read 1 Thessalonians 4 and Hebrews 4 together and a different picture emerges: the trumpet is not a fire alarm; it is the announcement that Sabbath has reached its fullness. Resurrection is not an escape hatch; it is the moment rest and rule finally embrace.

4. How the Escape Idea Actually Arose

For most of church history, believers expected one visible return of Christ, a bodily resurrection of the dead, a final judgment, and a renewed creation where heaven and earth are united.

The two-stage return—a secret removal followed by a later public appearing—arose much later, in the turbulence of the 1800s, when wars and rapid social change created deep anxiety. Over time, those ideas were printed in popular study Bibles and spread through conferences, media, and fiction until they felt ancient. But they are not ancient. They are not apostolic. They are not in the creeds.

The earliest believers faced persecution, plague, and empire. If they had been promised a secret evacuation, they would have clung to it. Instead, they prepared for endurance and resurrection.

5. Why Escape Theology Weakens the Bride

Beliefs form postures. Posture shapes preparation.

If you believe you are leaving at any minute: you focus on survival, not stewardship; you see suffering as interruption, not refinement; you watch headlines more than you watch your heart; you quietly assume responsibility for the world's long-term health belongs to someone else.

If you believe the King is coming *here:* you care deeply about what you build and how you build it; you see trials as training for reigning; you invest in generations you may never meet; you live as if your labor in the Lord is not in vain.

Escape theology trains a Bride to pack her bags. Royal-arrival theology trains a Bride to prepare the house.

Formation Matrix – Escape vs. Royal Arrival

Dimension	Escape Theology	Royal-Arrival Theology
Final hope	"I'll get out of here"	"My King will return here; I'll be with Him as He restores all things"
Posture toward culture	Disengagement – "It's all burning anyway"	Engagement – sowing righteousness because the Lord will redeem His creation
Identity of the Church	Fragile remnant trying to survive	Prepared Bride and governing Ecclesia
Motivation for holiness	Fear of being left behind	Desire to be a pure Bride ready to stand beside a holy King
How headlines are read	Countdown to disappearance – fuels anxiety	Birth pangs of the Kingdom's fullness – fuels intercession and hope

Dimension	Escape Theology	Royal-Arrival Theology
View of resurrection	Functionally minimized	Central – bodily resurrection is the gateway to shared rule

---

Formation Truth

The Bride who does not flee is not naïve about shaking. She has read Matthew 24 and Revelation. She knows about wars, rumors, lawlessness, and pressure. But she also knows:

- *"He who endures to the end will be saved."*
- *"The meek shall inherit the earth."*
- *"The dwelling of God is with humanity."*

Her hope is not escape. Her hope is union in a renewed world. And that hope changes everything–from how she prays to how she builds, from how she parents to how she leads.

---

6. The Bridal Shift: From Fleeing to Welcoming

Imagine a bride whose constant expectation is: *"Any minute, I'll be whisked away, and this world will be over."*

Now imagine another bride who knows: *"My Beloved is returning to live with me here. Our union will transform this place."*

Their behavior will be very different.

The first bride:

- Disconnects from long projects.
- Tolerates inner compromise–"Why bother? It's almost over."

- Reads every news story as a countdown.
- Sees holiness as optional and mission as extra.

The second bride:

- Lets the Spirit purify her because she expects to stand beside a holy King.
- Learns responsibility, because she expects to share His rule.
- Invests in people and places, because she knows they have a future.
- Sees holiness as preparation and mission as normal life.

The Bride who does not flee is not naïve about shaking. She has read Matthew 24 and Revelation. She knows about wars, rumors, lawlessness, pressure. But she also knows:

- *"He who endures to the end will be saved."*
- *"The meek shall inherit the earth."*
- *"The dwelling of God is with humanity."*

Her hope is not escape. Her hope is union in a renewed world.

7. You Were Not Wrong. You Were Early.

If you have believed in an escape for years, hear this clearly: you were not foolish. You were not faithless. You were comforted by something many sincere leaders taught you in turbulent times.

But comfort is not the same as covenant clarity.

This is not about shame. It is about maturity.

A child needs to be told, *"It will be okay."* An heir needs to be told, *"Stand your ground. You have a kingdom to inherit."*

You are not being scolded. You are being invited into your real role.

8. A New Confession for a Prepared Bride

Let this be the shift in your own mouth:

I am not waiting to flee the earth. I am preparing to welcome my King.

I am not scanning the sky for an escape signal. I am tending the oil in my lamp for His arrival.

The trumpet is not a panic alarm. It is the announcement of His public reign.

I will be caught up to greet Him, and I will return with Him in resurrection life.

I am not afraid of the days ahead. I am being formed for them.

I am the Bride who does not flee. I am the Bride who stands, so that when He comes, He finds faith on the earth.

The Five Refining Separations: Matthew 24–25 as Formation Architecture

Before the city of God appears in Revelation, Jesus describes the refining process that forms the people who will inhabit it. Matthew 24–25 unfolds as five progressive separations that reveal the true condition of the heart and prepare a people for the life of the age to come. Each separation exposes a different dimension of covenant formation.

1. Loyalty – The Faithful and the Unfaithful Servant (Matthew 24:45–51)

Jesus begins with loyalty in the hidden place. Two servants are given responsibility while the master is away. One remains faithful. The other abuses authority and begins living for himself. The separation reveals a fundamental truth: formation begins with loyalty when no one is watching.

2. Readiness – The Wise and the Foolish Virgins (Matthew 25:1–13)

The second separation moves from loyalty to readiness. Ten virgins wait for the bridegroom. Five prepare oil. Five assume there will be time later. When the bridegroom arrives unexpectedly, the difference becomes visible. The wise enter the celebration. The unprepared remain outside. Oil cannot be borrowed. The Bride must personally carry oil.

3. Stewardship – The Servants and the Talents (Matthew 25:14–30)

The third separation concerns stewardship. A master entrusts resources to his servants. Two multiply what was entrusted. One buries what he received out of fear. The issue is not equal capacity but faithful multiplication. Formation requires active participation in what God has entrusted.

4. Compassion – The Sheep and the Goats (Matthew 25:31-46)

The fourth separation reveals embodied covenant love. Nations are gathered before the Son of Man. The dividing line appears surprisingly simple: feeding the hungry, welcoming the stranger, clothing the vulnerable, visiting the sick and imprisoned. The King declares that what was done for "the least of these" was done for Him. Formation moves beyond belief into lived mercy.

5. Alignment – The Life of the Age to Come (Matthew 25:46)

The final separation reveals ultimate alignment. Jesus concludes: *"And these will go away into kolasis aiōnios, but the righteous into zōē aiōnios."* Two destinies appear—one life aligned with the coming age, one life subject to the corrective judgment of that age.

The entire sequence of refinements has been revealing who is aligned with the life of the Kingdom.

Refinement	What Is Revealed
Faithful Servant	Loyalty in hidden responsibility
Ten Virgins	Readiness—personal oil capacity
Talents	Stewardship—faithful multiplication
Sheep and Goats	Compassion—embodied covenant love
Final Separation	Alignment—participation in the life of the age to come

Jesus is not merely warning about judgment. He is revealing the formation process through which a people become ready for the Kingdom. The Bride who does not flee allows herself to be refined through every one of these separations—loyalty, readiness, stewardship, compassion, and alignment—until she stands as a people fully prepared for the King's arrival.

For Leaders & Owners – Reflection Box

For Leaders & Owners:

- Where has "it's all going to burn anyway" quietly shaped how you treat your staff, clients, or community?
- What decisions have you postponed because you hoped time—or the rapture—would make them unnecessary?
- If you really believed Jesus is coming *here* to reign, what is one way you would lead your company or team differently this year?
- Who on your team needs to hear a different story from your mouth—a story of building with the King, not waiting to flee?

Formation Practices

Inner Practice – Trade escape for engagement. Set aside 20-30 minutes with a journal and write honestly: *Where am I secretly hoping God will get me out instead of forming me to stand?* Name specific areas—marriage, parenting, finances, leadership. Ask the Spirit to show you one place where He is inviting you to stay and grow instead of plan your exit.

Bodily Practice – Practice presence in pressure. This week, when you feel overwhelmed by news or circumstances, instead of doomscrolling or shutting down, stop for three slow breaths and quietly say: *"You are coming here."* Let your body feel that sentence. Notice how it changes your posture.

Relational Practice – One conversation of responsibility. Identify one relationship where you have been waiting for things to "blow over" instead of owning your part—an employee, a colleague, a family member. Schedule a real conversation. Go into it with this heart: *I am not trying to* *escape discomfort. I am here to walk this through like someone who expects Jesus to reign here.*

Leadership Practice – One long-term act of faithfulness. Choose one concrete decision in your business or work that reflects long-term stewardship instead of short-term relief—investing in a younger leader, addressing a dysfunctional policy, making a quality upgrade you've delayed. Do it as an act of worship, consciously saying: *"I believe this matters to You, Jesus."*

---

9. The Practical Implications for Every Sphere

The shift from escape theology to royal-arrival theology does not only affect your prayer life. It reshapes how you engage every sphere of life.

In parenting: Escape theology says, "Protect your kids from the world until Jesus comes." Royal-arrival theology says, "Equip your children to carry the King's authority into the world He is redeeming." The first produces sheltered believers who are unprepared for real life. The second produces resilient, rooted sons and daughters who know who they are and whose they are.

In education: Escape theology says, "Christian education is a bunker where we keep our children safe from secular influence." Royal-arrival theology says, "Education—all education—is a domain where the King's truth can be explored and applied." This doesn't mean every Christian should attend a Christian school. It means every Christian student should carry Ecclesia identity into whatever classroom they enter.

In business: Escape theology says, "Make enough money to survive and give to missions until Jesus comes." Royal-arrival theology says, "Build enterprises that reflect the King's justice, generosity, and creativity—because what you build with Him will matter when He arrives." This transforms business from a necessary evil into a Kingdom vocation.

In politics and civic engagement: Escape theology says, "The world is going to hell—why bother?" Royal-arrival theology says, "The meek shall inherit the earth, so we engage the systems of the world as stewards of the Kingdom's justice and mercy." Not with triumphalism—with humble, faithful presence.

In art and culture: Escape theology produces art that is either escapist or apocalyptic. Royal-arrival theology produces art that is incarnational—rooted in the beauty, pain, and hope of a world that is being renewed. It produces stories, music, and visual art that reflect the truth: God is not abandoning creation. He is redeeming it.

10. The Sabbath Lens: Rest as the Ultimate Anti-Escape

There is one more dimension that deserves attention: the connection between royal-arrival theology and Sabbath rest.

Escape theology is, at its core, restless. It is always scanning, always anxious, always watching for the exit. It cannot truly rest because it does not believe the future is secure.

Royal-arrival theology is, at its core, restful. Not passive—restful. It trusts that the King has all authority, that His return is certain, and that the labor we do in Him is not in vain. That trust produces a different kind of rest—not the rest of disengagement, but the rest of confidence.

Hebrews 4 calls this *"the Sabbath rest that remains for the people of God."* It is the rest of a finished work—not finished because we have done everything, but finished because He has secured everything.

When you operate from that rest:

- You don't strive from anxiety. You work from overflow.
- You don't build from fear of loss. You build from the security of the Kingdom.
- You don't rest because you're exhausted. You rest because you trust.

The Bride who does not flee is also the Bride who truly rests. She has heard the King say, *"It is finished."* She has seen the empty tomb. She knows the end of the story. And from that knowledge, she builds, serves, leads, and loves—not with the frantic energy of escape, but with the settled authority of a people whose future is as certain as the One who holds it.

Selah – Pause Here

Take a moment and ask: *Have I secretly hoped to be rescued from the very places God asked me to take responsibility?*

Let specific situations come to mind–family, work, city.

Pray: *Jesus, I lay down my hope of escape, and I ask You to teach me how to stand with You instead.*

Selah – Pause Again

Imagine Jesus returning–not to snatch you out, but to walk into the very places you lead. Would you feel proud to show Him what you've built, or relieved that it's over?

Pray: *King Jesus, teach me to build now in a way I will not be ashamed of when I stand beside You.*

---

11. The Revelation 21 Vision: The End That Reshapes the Beginning

The clearest single verse that demolishes escape theology is Revelation 21:3: *"Behold, the dwelling of God is with humanity. He will dwell with them, and they shall be His people, and God Himself will be with them as their God."*

Notice: God does not take humanity away to heaven. He brings heaven to earth. He dwells *with them.* The final destiny is not disembodied souls floating in a celestial elsewhere. It is a renewed creation where God and humanity live together in the city that comes *down from heaven.*

The New Jerusalem does not ascend from earth. It descends from heaven. Heaven comes here. God moves in. The marriage is consummated not in escape, but in union–embodied, located, real.

This vision reshapes everything:

- **Your body matters.** It will be resurrected, not discarded. The hope of the gospel is not the escape of the soul but the redemption of the whole person–body, soul, and spirit.

- **The earth matters.** It will be renewed, not destroyed. The fire Peter describes in 2 Peter 3 is purification, not annihilation—the same way gold is refined by fire but not eliminated by it.

- **Your work matters.** Isaiah 65 describes the new creation in terms of building, planting, and enjoying the fruit of labor. Work is not a curse that ends at the rapture. It is a gift that continues in glory.

- **Relationships matter.** The nations walk in the light of the city. Kings bring their glory into it. The tree of life bears fruit for the healing of the nations. The relational fabric of creation is not burned away—it is healed and completed.

When you let Revelation 21 rewrite your eschatology, everything changes. You stop treating this world as a waiting room and start treating it as a construction site. You stop hoping to leave and start preparing to receive the One who is coming *here.*

12. The Courage to Build in the Shaking

The final word for this chapter is about courage.

Royal-arrival theology does not promise that life will be easy. It promises that life will be meaningful. The same Jesus who told us about the marriage supper also told us about tribulation, persecution, and the love of many growing cold.

The Bride who does not flee is not a Bride who ignores difficulty. She is a Bride who faces difficulty with a different posture—not the posture of someone trying to survive until evacuation, but the posture of someone preparing the house for the King.

That posture requires courage:

- The courage to invest when others are retreating.

- The courage to build when others say, "It's all going down."

- The courage to stay when others are looking for the exit.

- The courage to raise children with vision for the future when the headlines scream despair.

- The courage to lead your business with generational intentionality when the market rewards only quarterly thinking.

This courage is not manufactured by positive thinking. It is grounded in theology—in the unshakeable conviction that the King is coming, that His Kingdom cannot be shaken, and that every act of faithful obedience will be rewarded when He arrives.

The Bride does not flee. She builds. She stands. She prepares the house. And when the trumpet sounds, she does not grab her bag. She opens the front door and says:

Welcome home, my King. We've been getting ready for You.

Activation Prayer / Declaration

I am not waiting to flee the earth. I am preparing to welcome my King.

I am not scanning the sky for an escape signal. I am tending the oil in my lamp for His arrival.

The trumpet is not a panic alarm. It is the announcement of His public reign.

I will be caught up to greet Him, and I will return with Him in resurrection life.

I am not afraid of the days ahead. I am being formed for them.

I am the Bride who does not flee. I am the Bride who stands, so that when He comes, He finds faith on the earth.

Scripture for Meditation

- 1 Thessalonians 4:16–17 – "Caught up to meet the Lord" – royal arrival language
- Matthew 24:37–39 – "As in the days of Noah" – who was actually taken?
- Hebrews 4:9–11 – "There remains a Sabbath rest for the people of God"

- Revelation 21:3 – "The dwelling of God is with humanity"
- 2 Peter 3:13 – "We are looking forward to a new heaven and a new earth"
- Luke 18:8 – "When the Son of Man comes, will He find faith on the earth?"

Challenge – Before You Step Into the Next Chapter

Ask yourself one question and write down your honest answer: *If Jesus told me He was returning in fifty years instead of tomorrow, would I lead any differently?*

If the answer is yes—then escape theology has been shaping your decisions more than you realized. Let the royal-arrival truth begin to reshape your posture, your plans, and your preparation.

The next chapter is a declaration—a sovereignty decree for the Bride who has decided to stand. Come ready to speak it, not just read it.

Eleven

THE SOVEREIGNTY DECLARATION OF THE PREPARED BRIDE

Once the lie of escape is broken, something must fill the space it occupied. If fear is removed without installing identity, the heart drifts. This chapter is not another argument. It is a decree – a way for the Bride to stand up inside herself and say what is now true.

For years, a different story has been writing itself on the nervous system of the Church. A story of fragility. A story of countdown clocks and exit signs. A story that says, *You are too small for what is coming. Your only hope is removal.* That story trained the body to brace – shoulders tight, eyes scanning, heart waiting for bad news, faith tied to headlines.

Heaven calls the Bride something else. Not fragile. Not fleeing. Prepared. This chapter is meant to be spoken, not just read.

Story Window – The Woman Who Stopped Watching the Sky

Grace was the executive director of a faith-based housing nonprofit in a mid-sized Southern city. She had led the organization through two recessions, a pandemic, and a season when donations dried up so badly she paid staff out of her own savings for three months.

She loved Jesus. She also carried a quiet, low-grade dread she never named. Every time a new headline broke – war, economic instability, natural disaster – something inside her whispered, *This is it. It's all about to end. Why am I pouring so much into buildings that won't matter?*

She didn't realize how deeply that script was running until a board meeting where the team proposed a ten-year strategic plan. One of the board members, a retired developer, laid out a vision for permanent supportive housing that would serve three generations. He spoke with conviction: "We're building something that will outlast all of us."

Grace felt her chest tighten. She heard herself say, almost before she could stop it, "I just don't know if we'll have ten years."

The room went quiet. The developer looked at her gently and said, "Grace, do you believe Jesus is coming back to *destroy* this city, or to *redeem* it?"

She couldn't answer. Not because she didn't know the theology. Because she realized her theology said one thing and her nervous system said another. Her body had been trained by decades of rapture-countdown preaching to brace, not build. To survive, not steward. To scan the sky, not cultivate the ground.

That night, alone in her office, she opened her Bible to Isaiah 65 – *They shall build houses and inhabit them; they shall plant vineyards and eat their fruit.* Then to Jeremiah 29 – *Build houses and live in them; plant gardens and eat what they produce... seek the welfare of the city.* Then to Revelation 21 – *Behold, I am making all things new.*

Not *all new things.* All things *new.*

Something shifted. She began to weep – not from grief, but from the weight of years spent bracing instead of building. She prayed, *Lord, forgive me. I have been leading from an evacuation mindset while telling people to have hope.*

Over the next year, Grace didn't just approve the ten-year plan. She became its fiercest advocate. She started speaking differently to donors: "We are building because the King is coming *here.* Our work is preparation for His reign, not a holding pattern until His rescue." Staff noticed the change. The atmosphere in the office shifted from noble endurance to purposeful joy. Volunteers stopped asking, "Does this even matter?" and started asking, "What else can we build?"

The nonprofit broke ground on its largest project yet – fifty-two units of permanent housing. On the wall of the first completed unit, Grace hung a small plaque: *We build because He is coming. – Revelation 21:5*

What This Shows Us

Escape theology trains the body to brace. Sovereignty theology trains the body to build. When a leader shifts from scanning the sky for evacuation to stewarding the ground for the King's arrival, everything beneath that leader shifts too — culture, investment, endurance, and hope.

Scripture Deep Dive — From Anxiety Posture to Authority Posture

Escape theology trains the body into a recognizable posture: shoulders tight, eyes scanning, heart waiting for bad news, faith tied to headlines. Sovereignty theology trains the body into a different posture: shoulders back, gaze lifted, heart anchored, faith tied to the King.

Sovereignty does not mean controlling events. It means knowing *whose* you are and where history is headed. A prepared Bride does not flinch every time the earth shakes. She remembers that her Bridegroom already holds all authority in heaven and on earth — Matthew 28:18.

Paul writes to the Thessalonians, "God has not destined us for wrath, but to obtain salvation through our Lord Jesus Christ" — 1 Thessalonians 5:9. That salvation is not extraction from the world. It is the full realization of what Christ purchased: a people standing with Him when He appears, radiant and unashamed.

The writer of Hebrews describes a kingdom that "cannot be shaken" — Hebrews 12:28. The shaking removes what is temporary. What remains is the Bride's inheritance. Her posture must match what she inherits: unshakable, because her King is unshakable.

Formation Matrix — Escape Posture vs. Sovereignty Posture

Dimension	Escape Posture	Sovereignty Posture
Body language	Shoulders tight, braced for impact	Shoulders back, settled in identity
Eye focus	Scanning headlines for countdown clues	Fixed on the King who holds all authority
Heart condition	Waiting for bad news	Anchored in covenant promise
Faith attachment	Tied to current events	Tied to the Lamb slain before the foundation
View of suffering	Interruption to escape from	Refinement that produces endurance

View of work	Temporary – "it's all going to burn"	Eternal – "my labor in the Lord is not in vain"
Leadership tone	Noble endurance, survival mode	Purposeful joy, building for the King's arrival
Prayer posture	"Get me out"	"Make me faithful"

Formation Truth

The Bride is not appointed to wrath. She is appointed to salvation – and salvation, in its fullest biblical sense, includes standing with the King at His appearing. Authority posture is not pretending difficulty does not exist. It is the settled conviction that no difficulty has the final word, because the One who holds the final word has already spoken it: "Behold, I am making all things new."

For Leaders & Owners – Reflection Box

- Where has "it's all going to burn anyway" quietly shaped how you treat your staff, clients, or community?
- What decisions have you postponed because you hoped time – or the rapture – would make them unnecessary?
- If you really believed Jesus is coming *here* to reign, what is one way you would lead your company or team differently this year?
- Who on your team needs to hear a different story from your mouth – a story of building with the King, not waiting to flee?

Formation Practices This Week

- **Inner –** *Trade escape for engagement.* Set aside 20–30 minutes with a journal and write honestly: "Where am I secretly hoping God will get me out instead of forming me to stand?" Name specific areas – marriage, parenting, finances, leadership. Ask the Spirit to show you one place where He is inviting you to stay and grow instead of plan your exit.
- **Bodily –** *Practice presence in pressure.* This week, when you feel overwhelmed by news or circumstances, instead of doomscrolling or shutting down, stop for three slow breaths and

quietly say, "You are coming *here*." Let your body feel that sentence. Notice how it changes your posture.

- **Relational** – *One conversation of responsibility.* Identify one relationship where you have been waiting for things to blow over instead of owning your part – an employee, a colleague, a family member. Schedule a real conversation. Go into it with this heart: "I am not trying to escape discomfort. I am here to walk this through like someone who expects Jesus to reign *here*."
- **Leadership** – *One long-term act of faithfulness.* Choose one concrete decision in your business or work that reflects long-term stewardship instead of short-term relief – investing in a younger leader, addressing a dysfunctional policy, making a quality upgrade you've delayed. Do it as an act of worship, consciously saying, "I believe this matters to You, Jesus."

Selah – Pause Here

Take a slow breath. Ask yourself: *If Jesus walked into my office, my home, my team meeting tomorrow – not to rescue me from it, but to evaluate what I've been building – would I feel proud to show Him? Or relieved that it's finally over?*

Let that question sit. Do not rush past it.

Pray: *King Jesus, teach me to build now in a way I will not be ashamed of when I stand beside You.*

Activation – Personal Sovereignty Declaration

Speak this slowly. Let each line land.

I am not appointed to fear. I am not appointed to panic. I am not watching the horizon for escape. I am watching for my King.

The trumpet is not an alarm of removal. It is the announcement of arrival. The clouds are not my hiding place. They are the backdrop of His unveiling.

I will be caught up to greet Him, and I will stand with Him as He sets all things in order. I will rise. I will be transformed. I will meet the Lord. And I will always be with Him.

I am not fragile in tribulation. I am refined in it. I am not a victim of the last days. I am a partner of the Coming One.

My hope is not in being removed from the earth, but in seeing the earth renewed under His reign. I do not despise this world. I expect it to be made new.

I renounce the belief that I am here to survive until evacuation. I embrace the truth that I am here to bear His image, to carry His authority, and to embody His love until He appears.

Pause there. Notice what is happening in you as you say it. Agreement is not just mental. Your body feels it.

Activation – Corporate Bridal Declaration

Now widen the lens. This is not just about one person. This is about a people.

We are not an anxious church, pacing the earth for an exit. We are the Bride of Christ, standing in our generation with oil in our lamps.

We are not appointed to wrath. We are appointed to salvation. We have been washed, we have been set apart, we have been declared righteous in the Name of Jesus.

We are not a footnote in history. We are the people in whom the new creation has already begun.

We are not spectators of the King's return. We are the ones who will greet Him, and reign with Him in a renewed creation.

We do not partner with fear. We partner with faith. We do not partner with despair. We partner with hope. We do not partner with lawlessness. We partner with holiness and love.

We declare that wars and shakings are not our countdown to disappearance, but the birth pangs of a world about to see its true King.

We refuse to call darkness final. We refuse to call brokenness permanent. We refuse to agree with any story that ends without the Lamb on the throne and the Bride by His side.

Challenge to the Reader

The declaration you just spoke broke something in the atmosphere around you – whether you felt it or not. But a declaration without understanding becomes a slogan. In the next chapter, the journey turns to a subtle and dangerous counterfeit: a version of spirituality that *sounds* like freedom but actually teaches the Bride to despise her own body, her own story, and the very world her King came to redeem. If the sovereignty declaration planted your feet on the ground, the next chapter will show you why *staying* on the ground – embodied, present, and participating – is itself an act of war against an ancient lie.

Scripture for Meditation

1 Thessalonians 5:1–11 · Hebrews 12:25–29 · Revelation 21:1–5 · Isaiah 65:17–25 · Jeremiah 29:4–7

TWELVE

THE FALSE ESCAPE: GNOSTIC IDENTITY VS. COVENANT PARTICIPATION

Not every deep spiritual phrase comes from the heart of God. Some of the most seductive ideas in the modern Church sound powerful, mystical, even revelatory – but they mirror an ancient heresy more than the gospel. They do not form a Bride who stands in her calling. They form a people trying to float away from embodiment, responsibility, and history.

This chapter puts two frameworks side by side: Gnostic escape identity and new-covenant embodied union with Christ – so the reader can feel, very clearly, what belongs to Jesus and what does not.

Story Window – The Pastor Who Floated Above His People

Darren was a worship leader turned senior pastor with a gift for language. His phrases were stunning – *"You are not of this density," "Your truest self has never been wounded," "Rise above the illusion of matter."* People left his services feeling elevated, weightless, almost transcendent. Social media clips of his messages went viral.

But something strange was happening in his congregation. People who were grieving were told their grief was "agreement with the material realm." A woman going through a brutal divorce was counseled to "remember her real self is untouched." A businessman struggling with ethical decisions at work was told, "Business is the lower realm – don't let it pollute your spirit."

The language sounded spiritual. The fruit was disconnection.

One Sunday, a visiting pastor – an older woman named Margaret who had spent thirty years in hospital chaplaincy – sat in the back row. She listened to Darren speak eloquently about the spirit transcending the body. Then she watched as a young mother, visibly shaking with postpartum depression, approached the prayer team. The prayer team member smiled gently and said, "Remember, your real self is beyond this. These emotions belong to the flesh."

The young mother walked away more alone than before.

After the service, Margaret asked Darren for coffee. She was direct. "Darren, what you're teaching is beautiful language wrapped around a very old lie. It's Gnosticism. And it's starving your people."

He was taken aback. "I'm teaching freedom. Transcendence. Identity in Christ."

"No," she said. "You're teaching *escape* from the incarnation. Jesus didn't float above human suffering. He walked into it. He wept. He bled. He ate fish after the resurrection. The gospel is not that we escape our bodies. It's that God entered one – permanently."

She opened her Bible to John 1:14 – *The Word became flesh and dwelt among us.* Then to 1 John 4:2 – *Every spirit that confesses that Jesus Christ has come in the flesh is from God.* Then to Romans 8:11 – *He who raised Christ from the dead will also give life to your mortal bodies through His Spirit who dwells in you.*

"The early Church had a test for false teaching," she said. "Does it confess that Christ came *in the flesh*? If a teaching makes you despise your body, dismiss your story, or detach from the world God is redeeming – it has failed the test."

Darren stared at his coffee for a long time. Then he said something Margaret didn't expect: "I think I've been preaching this because I'm trying to escape my own pain."

That confession was the beginning of a different kind of ministry – one where suffering was not bypassed but carried into the presence of a God who had suffered Himself.

What This Shows Us

Gnostic-flavored spirituality feels empowering because it lifts you above your pain. But the gospel does not lift you above your pain. It walks *into* your pain with you, transforms it, and redeems it – body, story, and all.

Any teaching that consistently makes believers detach from embodiment, responsibility, and real human connection has failed the test of 1 John 4:2.

Scripture Deep Dive – Incarnation: God's Final Word Against Escape

Gnosticism, in its many forms, carries a simple message under different clothes: spirit is good, matter is bad, and the goal is to escape the material realm by secret knowledge.

In some modern Christian circles, this has been baptized into phrases like: "I am not really from here" – meant as literal escape, not covenant belonging; or "I'm just a spirit being having a human experience" – meant as dismissal of the human, not honor of incarnation.

The apostolic gospel is profoundly different. It is not God rescuing disembodied souls out of a trash-heap world. It is God loving the world He made. The Word becoming flesh and dwelling among us. Jesus rising in a body that eats, walks, and bears scars. The promise of the resurrection of the *body*, not escape from it. A new heavens and new earth, not the abandonment of both.

If God believed matter was beneath Him, He would never have become human. Incarnation is God's loud *No* to every story that despises creation. The Son of God took on real flesh, walked in real dust, bore real pain, died a real death, rose with a real body. He did not merely appear as human. He became human. And He did not shed His humanity after the resurrection. He remains the God-Man.

That means: your body is not an inconvenience – it is a site of redemption. Your emotions, history, and relationships are not distractions – they are arenas for Christ's life to be formed in you. The future is not a disembodied cloud – it is a renewed creation where embodied people live face to face with God.

Formation Matrix – Gnostic Escape vs. Covenant Participation

Dimension	Gnostic Escape Identity	Covenant Participation
View of the body	Shell to transcend; "not the real me"	Temple of the Holy Spirit; site of redemption

View of suffering	Illusion to rise above	Arena where Christ's life is formed in us
View of history	Irrelevant; escape is the goal	Stage where God is actively redeeming
View of creation	Doomed material realm	Destined for renewal under Christ's reign
Relational posture	Detached superiority	Engaged compassion – weep with those who weep
Source of identity	Secret inner knowledge	Union with the incarnate, risen Christ
Test (1 John 4:2)	Does not confess Christ *in the flesh*	Confesses that Jesus Christ has come in the flesh
Fruit	Disconnection, spiritual elitism, dismissal of pain	Embodied love, real-world stewardship, hope

Formation Truth

The Bride's hope is resurrection and union – not absorption and disappearance. Covenant participation sends you *into* pain with comfort, *into* broken systems with wisdom, and teaches you to carry Christ in your body, not away from it. When Jesus says, "They are not of the world, just as I am not of the world" – John 17 – He is defining allegiance and origin of life, not commanding disdain for creation.

For Leaders & Owners – Reflection Box

- Have you used spiritual language to dismiss the weight of real problems in your business – telling yourself or your team, "This world isn't our home anyway"?
- In your leadership style, is there a split between your "spiritual life" and how you handle money, contracts, hiring, and conflict?
- Covenant identity insists that how you run your business *is* part of your worship. What shifts if you truly believe that?

Formation Practices This Week

- **Inner –** *Language audit.* This week, listen to the phrases you repeat about yourself and your world. Write down any that consistently pull you toward detachment: "This world isn't real," "My body doesn't matter," "I'm just passing through." For each one, ask: Does this make me more engaged with Jesus and His people, or more detached?
- **Bodily –** *Honor your incarnation.* Choose one act this week that honors your body as a temple, not a shell: rest when tired, eat nourishment instead of numbing, take a walk and thank God for the ground under your feet. Say as you do it: "Christ in me. I am in Christ."
- **Relational –** *Sit with someone in pain without fixing them.* Find someone who is grieving, struggling, or worn out. Do not quote transcendence. Sit with them. Listen. Weep if the Spirit leads. Embody the incarnation – God *with* us.
- **Leadership –** *Close the sacred-secular split.* In your next leadership decision, refuse to separate "spiritual" from "practical." Before signing a contract, making a hire, or approving a budget, pause and ask: "Lord, does this reflect Your character? Am I worshiping You in this decision?"

Selah – Pause Here

Ask yourself honestly: *Have my favorite spiritual phrases been pulling me closer to real people and real responsibility – or further away?*

There is no condemnation in the question. Only an invitation to return to the incarnate Christ – the One who did not float above the world but walked into it, bled in it, and rose from its grave.

Pray: *Jesus, You are the Word who became flesh. You did not escape creation. You entered it. Make me a Bride who participates, not a spectator who escapes.*

Activation – Confession Back Into Participation

Jesus, You are the Word who became flesh. You did not escape creation. You entered it.

I renounce every story that teaches me to despise my body, to despise this world, or to treat history as meaningless.

I receive Your truth: I am not of this world's rebellion, but I am sent into this world as Your own.

My life is hidden with You in God – not hidden from responsibility.

I embrace my body as a temple, my story as a place of redemption, my relationships as the field where Your love grows, and this creation as something You intend to renew.

Make me a Bride who participates, not a spectator who escapes. Make me an Ecclesia who stands, not a soul trying to float away.

Until You come, let my spirituality look like Yours – fully surrendered, fully embodied, fully given for the life of the world.

Challenge to the Reader

With escape theology dismantled and Gnostic identity exposed, a question rises: *If the Bride is not fleeing and not floating – what anchors her?* The answer has been hiding in the prayer she has recited a thousand times without hearing it. The next chapter cracks open the final line of the Lord's Prayer – "For Yours is the kingdom and the power and the glory forever" – and reveals it as the architectural beam that holds everything the Bride has learned in place.

Scripture for Meditation

John 1:14 · 1 John 4:1-3 · Romans 8:11 · Colossians 3:1-4 · John 17:14-18 · 2 Corinthians 4:7-12

THIRTEEN

FOR YOURS IS THE KINGDOM: THE DOXOLOGY THAT ANCHORS IDENTITY

The Lord's Prayer begins with alignment – *Our Father in heaven, hallowed be Your name* – and ends with a declaration: *For Yours is the kingdom and the power and the glory forever.* That last line is more than a liturgical flourish. It is a reset of ownership.

This chapter treats that doxology as an architectural beam – a sentence that, when truly carried, stabilizes how the Bride prays, how she sees herself, and how she stands in shaking.

Story Window – The CEO Who Prayed It and Meant It

Renee ran a health services company with 400 employees. She was known for sharp instincts and a steady hand in volatile markets. She also prayed the Lord's Prayer every morning – not as ritual, but as alignment.

One quarter, everything shifted. A regulatory change threatened to cut revenue by 30%. A key executive left for a competitor. Her largest client renegotiated terms that felt predatory. In the same month, her teenage son was hospitalized after a mental health crisis.

She sat in her car in the hospital parking lot at 1 a.m., trying to pray. The words that came were the ones she had spoken every morning for years: *For Yours is the kingdom.*

She stopped.

Yours. Not mine. Not the market's. Not the regulator's. Not the competitor's. Not even the crisis's. *Yours.*

She kept going: *And the power.* Not my willpower. Not my strategy. Not my networking ability. The power that raised Christ from the dead.

And the glory. Not my reputation. Not the company's brand. Not what my board thinks of me. The weight and radiance belong to Someone else.

Forever. Not "until this quarter ends." Not "until the next election." Not "until my son is better." Forever. Beyond my lifetime. Beyond this company's existence. Beyond this crisis.

She realized she had been praying those words for years without letting them touch the places where she was actually terrified. That night, in the hospital parking lot, she finally let them in.

Over the next months, Renee led differently. Not with less urgency – with less panic. She made hard decisions about restructuring without being paralyzed by fear of losing people's approval. She told her board, "We are going to do this with integrity, even if it costs us short-term." She stopped checking her phone compulsively for market updates and instead started her mornings with ten minutes of silence and that same prayer – this time letting each word land like a stake in the ground.

Her son recovered slowly. The company survived – leaner, but healthier. And Renee carried a different weight. Not the weight of an empire she had to hold together, but the lightness of a woman who had placed her empire back in the hands of the One it belonged to.

What This Shows Us

The doxology is not decoration at the end of a prayer. It is the architectural beam that holds everything in place. When a leader actually means "Yours is the kingdom," they stop living like the weight of the world is on their shoulders – and start living like the weight of the world is on the throne of the One who cannot be shaken.

Scripture Deep Dive – The Seven Movements and the Final Anchor

Seen as a whole, the Lord's Prayer moves in seven deliberate stages:

1. **Identity** – *Our Father.* The prayer begins with belonging.
2. **Alignment** – *Hallowed be Your name.* Worship recenters everything.
3. **Authority** – *Your kingdom come, Your will be done.* Submission precedes request.

4. **Provision** – *Give us this day our daily bread.* Daily dependence, not hoarding.
5. **Cleansing** – *Forgive us... as we forgive.* Mercy given and received.
6. **Protection** – *Lead us not into temptation, but deliver us from evil.* Honest need for covering.
7. **Sovereignty** – *For Yours is the kingdom and the power and the glory forever.* Everything returns to the Owner.

The last line does not erase the requests. It frames them. It says, in effect: "I am a child talking to my Father. I have aligned with His name and will. I have asked for what I need. I have confessed my sin and released others. I have asked for protection. Now – I leave all of this in the hands of the One whose kingdom, power, and glory are secure beyond my lifetime."

That is how a Bride prays. Boldly, honestly, and then with open hands.

The Three Declarations Within the Doxology

Kingdom – Who Really Governs?

When the Bride says "Yours is the kingdom," she is confessing: The story does not belong to hell. The story does not belong to empires. The story does not belong to fear. The story belongs to *You.* This keeps the anointed heart from manipulating God with plans, panicking when things do not follow a script, or placing identity in outcomes.

Power – Who Really Makes Things Move?

"Yours is the power" acknowledges: "I am not the source of spiritual effectiveness. My eloquence, discipline, or gifting do not produce transformation. All true power for change – healing, deliverance, awakening, endurance – flows from You." For a Bride that has just renounced escapist passivity, this line is crucial. She is called to *participate,* not to *perform.* She carries authority, but not as independent power. She carries delegated power from a King whose strength does not run out.

Glory – Whose Reputation Is at Stake?

"Yours is the glory" surrenders the need to be the hero of the story, to receive credit for every breakthrough, or to protect image if God leads through paths that look weak. If He answers quickly, glory is His. If He answers slowly, glory is His. This fractures the subtle ministry-brand mindset. The Bride is not trying to build a name. She is carrying one.

Forever – Not a Season, a Reality

"Forever" is not poetic filler. It is a time word that breaks the Bride out of time-limited panic. No regime change in heaven is coming. No crisis on earth dethrones Him. No news cycle rewrites His ownership. In an age of rapid upheaval, saying "forever" over His kingdom, power, and glory calms the nervous system. The Bride starts living like everything hangs on an eternal King who has already outlived every empire and will outlive every one to come.

Formation Matrix – The Doxology as Identity Architecture

Doxology Element	What It Surrenders	What It Establishes	Bride Formation Effect
Kingdom	My plans, my empire, my control	His government over life and future	Stops building private kingdoms
Power	My strength, strategy, willpower	His healing, delivering, sustaining power	Shifts from performance to participation
Glory	My reputation, platform, brand	His visibility through surrendered lives	Breaks the need to be seen
Forever	My panic, my countdown, my timeline	His eternal stability	Calms the nervous system

Formation Truth

As a leader or owner, praying "Yours is the kingdom" is not a warm devotional moment – it is actively laying down the illusion that your company, platform, or position is your private empire. Each time you pray it, you hand Him the steering wheel of your strategy, not just the language of your prayers.

For Leaders & Owners – Reflection Box

- When you pray "Yours is the kingdom," do you mean it about your business? Your investments? Your retirement plan?
- Where have you treated power as something you generate rather than something delegated to you?
- Is your leadership building *your* name or carrying *His*?
- What would shift if you genuinely believed "forever" – that His kingdom outlasts every market cycle, every political upheaval, every personal failure?

Formation Practices This Week

- **Inner** – *Pray the doxology with your real fears.* Each morning this week, pray "For Yours is the kingdom and the power and the glory forever" – and after each word, insert the specific area where you are most tempted to take control. "Yours is the kingdom – over my finances. Yours is the power – over my son's health. Yours is the glory – over my reputation."
- **Bodily** – *Open your hands.* During prayer this week, physically open your palms upward as you say the doxology. Let your body practice releasing what your mind still grips.
- **Relational** – *Name someone else's glory.* In one conversation this week, intentionally credit someone else for a win that you could have claimed. Watch what happens in your heart when you release the glory.
- **Leadership** – *Audit your empire.* Ask one trusted advisor: "Where does it look like I'm building my own kingdom instead of stewarding His?" Listen without defending.

Selah – Pause Here

Before you move forward, sit with the Lord quietly. Not with calculations. With honesty.

Pray: *Father, Yours is the kingdom. Not mine. Not the enemy's. Yours is the government over my life, my calling, my city, and my future. Yours is the power. Not my strength, not my strategy, not my willpower. You are the One who heals, delivers, saves, sustains, and raises the dead. Yours is the glory. Not my name, not my reputation, not my platform. Let my life increase Your visibility, not mine. And this is not temporary. Not just true when things go well. Not just true when I feel it. Yours is the kingdom, and the power, and the glory, forever.*

Challenge to the Reader

The doxology anchored identity. But identity alone does not complete formation. The Bride must also learn to read the book that most Christians avoid or misread – Revelation. Not as a fear manual. Not as a prophecy chart. As a *formation blueprint.* The next chapter opens the Apocalypse not as escape literature but as the King's personal formation curriculum for a people He is preparing to reign with Him.

Scripture for Meditation

Matthew 6:9–13 · 1 Chronicles 29:11–13 · Psalm 145:13 · Daniel 4:34–35 · Revelation 11:15

FOURTEEN

REVELATION AS FORMATION BLUEPRINT

The book of Revelation has been treated as many things: a puzzle, a threat, a prophecy chart, a source of nightmares. For many believers, it is the book they skip because it feels too frightening, too strange, or too controversial.

But what if Revelation is not primarily a timeline of events – but a formation blueprint? What if the King wrote it not to terrify His Bride, but to train her?

Story Window – The Elder Who Stopped Being Afraid of Revelation

Pastor James had avoided teaching Revelation for twenty-three years. Every time someone in his congregation asked about it, he'd deflect: "That's a complex book – we'll get to it someday." Privately, his reasons were simpler. The book scared him. Every framework he'd been given – pre-trib charts, Left Behind timelines, beast-identification games – left him with dread, not hope.

Then his church went through a two-year season of intense difficulty. A building project collapsed financially. A beloved staff member was caught in moral failure. Three families left after a painful congregational conflict. The remaining members were exhausted and confused.

One night during prayer, an image came to him: seven lampstands, each flickering at different intensities. He recognized it immediately – the opening vision of Revelation. And he heard something in his spirit he hadn't expected: *I walk among the lampstands. I see every church. I know their condition. And I am not abandoning any of them.*

That week, he opened Revelation 1-3 for the first time as a pastor and read Jesus' letters to the seven churches – not as historical documents or prophetic puzzles, but as formation letters from a Bridegroom inspecting His Bride.

He found in those chapters a Jesus who was tender with the faithful, honest about compromise, fierce against mixture, and relentlessly committed to restoration. Every letter ended with a promise for those who overcome — not for those who escape.

He began a teaching series that Sunday. "Revelation," he told his congregation, "is not a horror movie. It is a love story and a formation journey — from garden beginnings to city glory, from mixture to union, from compromise to crown."

The atmosphere in the church shifted. People who had dreaded Revelation began reading it with highlighters instead of anxious hearts. They saw themselves in the seven churches — the love that had cooled, the faithfulness under pressure, the tolerance of things Christ was confronting. They began to pray Revelation's promises over themselves. And for the first time, they read the ending not as an evacuation plan, but as a wedding announcement.

What This Shows Us

Revelation was written to form the Bride, not to frighten her. When it is read as a formation blueprint — where every seal, trumpet, and bowl corresponds to spiritual processes the Church walks through — it becomes one of the most practical and hopeful books in Scripture.

Scripture Deep Dive — Reading Revelation as Formation, Not Escape

Revelation 1 opens with Jesus walking among His churches — not watching from a distance. He is involved, inspecting, and speaking directly to their spiritual conditions. The seven letters in chapters 2-3 reveal that the King is not primarily interested in eschatological timelines. He is interested in the interior condition of His people.

The sequence that follows — seals, trumpets, bowls — can be read not just as future events but as *formation stages*: layers of shaking that expose what is truly anchored and what is not. The conflict chapters reveal how the Bride learns to discern voices, loyalties, and pressures. The harvest passages show maturity forming. Babylon's fall reveals the collapse of false trusts. And the wedding of the Lamb – Revelation 19 – shows a Bride adorned not in escape-anxiety but in the righteous acts of the saints.

When this pattern is overlaid onto the believer's life, a personal formation map emerges: Letters (self-examination) → Seals/Trumpets/Bowls (shaking and purification) → Conflict (discernment under pressure) → Harvest (maturity) → Babylon's fall (release from false systems) → Marriage (union and adornment) → City (habitation with God).

Formation Matrix – The Seven Churches as Spiritual Conditions

Church	Strength	Weakness	Christ's Command	Overcoming Promise
Ephesus	Hard work, endurance, doctrinal discernment	Left their first love	Remember, repent, return to first works	Eat from the Tree of Life in paradise
Smyrna	Faithful under persecution, spiritual riches	Impending suffering	Do not fear; be faithful unto death	Crown of life; no harm from second death
Pergamum	Holding fast to Jesus' Name in hostile territory	Tolerating false teaching	Repent, or I will fight against them	Hidden manna; white stone with new name
Thyatira	Love, service, faith, growing works	Tolerating Jezebel influence	Zero tolerance for spiritual seduction	Authority over nations; the morning star

Sardis	Reputation of life and success	Spiritual deadness beneath reputation	Wake up; strengthen what remains	Clothed in white; name not erased
Philadelphia	True faithfulness; kept the Word	Limited power, opposition	Hold fast what you have	Made a pillar in God's temple
Laodicea	Material wealth, self-confidence	Lukewarmness; blind to true poverty	Buy gold refined by fire; open the door	Sit with Jesus on His throne

Formation Truth

Revelation is not just what will happen. It is how God *finishes* what He started – in the earth and in the reader. The Bride who reads Revelation as formation will find herself in every chapter – in the churches being inspected, in the shakings being refined, in the conflict being trained, and in the wedding being adorned.

For Leaders & Owners – Reflection Box

- Which of the seven churches most describes your organization right now? Your leadership? Your own heart?
- Where has "Babylon" – the seduction of false security, false systems, or false worship – found a seat in your business culture?
- If Revelation is a formation journey, what stage do you sense God is walking you through right now: inspection, shaking, conflict, harvest, or preparation for union?

Formation Practices This Week

- **Inner** – *Read Revelation 2-3 as a personal letter.* Read each of the seven letters this week, one per day. After each, ask: "Lord, what in this letter is for *me* right now?" Journal what He highlights.

- **Bodily –** *Fast one meal and read Revelation 21-22.* Replace one meal this week with reading the final two chapters of Revelation. Let the imagery of the city, the river, and the Tree of Life wash over your imagination. Notice how different it feels from the fear-based Revelation you may have been taught.
- **Relational –** *Share one promise from the seven churches.* Choose one "overcoming promise" from the letters and share it with someone this week – a friend, a spouse, a team member. Speak it as blessing, not as theory.
- **Leadership –** *Evaluate your lampstand.* Ask your leadership team: "If Jesus walked into our organization and wrote us a letter like He did the seven churches, what would He commend? What would He confront?" Let the conversation be honest.

Selah – Pause Here

The Lamb who was slain is the same Lamb who sits on the throne. The Jesus who washed feet is the same Jesus whose eyes are like fire. Do not separate His tenderness from His authority. The formation of the Bride requires both.

Pray: *Jesus, You are the One revealed in this book. You walk among Your churches. You sit on the throne. You open the seals. You fight for truth. You cleanse, confront, and comfort. Let this blueprint form me. Search me like You searched the seven churches. Show me the throne in every shaking. Make me part of a Bride who is not afraid of Revelation, but who reads it as a love story and a formation journey – moving from garden beginnings to city glory, from mixture to union, from compromise to crown.*

Challenge to the Reader

If Revelation shows how God forms a *corporate* Bride, the next chapter reveals that His formation plan has always been wider than most expected. When the Spirit was poured out on "all flesh," God meant *all.* Including the ones the Church has most often overlooked – the ones whose bodies and brains don't match the world's expectations. The Bride cannot afford to miss her most radiant members simply because they don't fit a stage.

Scripture for Meditation

Revelation 1:9–20 · Revelation 2–3 · Revelation 19:6–9 · Revelation 21:1–7 · Revelation 22:1–5

FIFTEEN

THE SPIRIT POURED OUT ON ALL FLESH: THE OVERLOOKED VESSELS

When God said He would pour out His Spirit on all flesh, He meant exactly that. Not just on preachers. Not just on the eloquent. Not just on the socially seamless. *All flesh.* Sons and daughters. Old and young. Servants and those the world never puts on a stage.

If the Bride only recognizes the polished, she will miss some of her most radiant members.

Story Window – The Boy Who Worshiped Without Words

Elijah was seven years old, autistic, and non-speaking. He communicated through a letterboard and through patterns – the way he rocked when music played, the way he pressed his forehead against the window when it rained, the way his entire body stilled when someone prayed with genuine sincerity.

His grandmother, Diane, brought him to church every Sunday. Most weeks, the children's ministry team smiled politely and placed him in the back corner with headphones and a coloring sheet. They were kind. They were also lost.

One Sunday, the worship team began a spontaneous song – unscripted, unhurried, just voices and a single guitar. The atmosphere shifted. Adults wept. Some knelt. And Elijah stood up in the children's room, walked to the door, pushed it open, and walked into the sanctuary.

Nobody stopped him. His grandmother watched, holding her breath.

He walked to the front of the room, stood directly before the worship team, and lifted both hands. His body, which usually moved in restless rhythms, became completely still. Tears streamed down his face. He did not make a sound. But every person in the room felt it – a weight of worship that none of them could manufacture.

The worship leader later said, "I've been doing this for twenty years. I have never felt the presence of God that thick. And the person who carried it into the room was a child who cannot speak."

After the service, Diane sat with him and his letterboard. She spelled out: *What did you feel in there?*

He pointed, letter by letter: *H-E W-A-S T-H-E-R-E. I C-O-U-L-D S-E-E H-I-M.*

She wept.

From that day, the church stopped placing Elijah in the back corner. They began including him – not as a project, but as a member. A participant. A vessel. They learned to watch his body for cues others couldn't read. When he became agitated during a service, they didn't assume it was sensory overload – they began asking, *"Is something shifting in the atmosphere that he can feel and we can't?"*

Within a year, the congregation's understanding of "all flesh" had been permanently expanded – not by theology alone, but by a child who worshiped with his whole body when words were never an option.

What This Shows Us

The Spirit was poured out on *all* flesh – all bodies, all neural wiring, all capacities. The Bride cannot afford to treat differently-abled members as ministry projects only. They are co-heirs. They may carry intercession, perception, joy, purity, or sensitivity to the Spirit's movement that the rest of the body desperately needs.

Scripture Deep Dive – All Flesh Means All

"In the last days, I will pour out My Spirit on all flesh..." – Joel 2:28, quoted by Peter in Acts 2:17.

God specifically names: sons and daughters – both genders; young and old – every generation; servants – those at the bottom of social ladders. If that logic is extended, "all flesh" includes all bodies, all neural wiring, all capacities. The outpouring is not limited to those who can stand behind a microphone.

It will land on children who rock and hum in the back row. On adults who never make eye contact but feel the room shift before anyone else does. On individuals whose language is movement, touch, or sound more than sentences.

Common mistakes the Church makes: assuming lack of speech equals lack of understanding; aiming teaching far below actual comprehension; treating them as objects of pity, not subjects of destiny; using them as illustrations of weakness rather than as actual contributors. Yet again and again, when given tools like letterboards, alternative communication, or patient presence, many non-speaking individuals reveal theological insight, emotional depth, and acute spiritual awareness. The problem was never their spirit. It was the Church's assumptions.

Formation Matrix – The Church's Assumptions vs. Heaven's Questions

The Church Often Asks	Heaven Asks
What's wrong with this person?	Who is this, and what have I placed in them?
How do we manage their needs?	How do we receive their gifts?
Can they understand the sermon?	What are they perceiving that no one else can?
Where do we put them so they don't disrupt?	Where do we place them so they can shine?
Will they ever be "normal"?	What facet of Jesus do they carry?

Formation Truth

Parents often ask through tears, "What's wrong with my child?" Heaven asks a different question: "Who is this, and what have I placed in them?" The Bride needs to be wide enough, deep enough, and humble enough to receive what God is pouring out on *all flesh* – including the flesh the world never puts on a stage.

For Leaders & Owners – Reflection Box

- In your organization, who are the "overlooked vessels" – people whose contributions are invisible because they don't fit the expected mold?
- Have you built systems that only recognize and reward people who communicate and perform like you?
- What would shift if you began asking about every team member: "What facet of excellence do they carry that I haven't yet learned to see?"

Formation Practices This Week

- **Inner** – *Repent for narrow categories.* Ask the Spirit: "Where have I unconsciously narrowed 'all flesh' to 'people like me'?" Let Him show you specific faces, specific assumptions. Repent without defending.
- **Bodily** – *Spend time with someone whose body works differently.* This week, be present – not as a helper, but as a learner – with someone who is differently abled. Watch. Listen. Ask God: "What are You showing me through them?"
- **Relational** – *Include, don't just accommodate.* Identify one way your family, church, or team can move from *accommodating* a differently-abled person to *including* them – not as a project, but as a participant with something to offer.
- **Leadership** – *Redesign one process for wider access.* Choose one meeting, one event, or one communication channel in your organization and ask: "Who is currently excluded from contributing here, not because they lack capacity, but because the format doesn't fit them?" Change the format.

Selah – Pause Here

Think of someone you know – perhaps someone in your family, your church, or your workplace – whose body or brain does not cooperate with the world's expectations.

Now ask God: *What do You see when You look at them? What have You placed inside them that I have not yet learned to receive?*

Let His answer change how you see.

Activation – A Blessing Over the Overlooked

Lord, You promised to pour out Your Spirit on all flesh. I bring before You every child, every adult, whose body or brain does not cooperate with the world's expectations.

I repent for every time we have underestimated them, spoken down to them, or treated them as projects instead of partners.

I bless the autistic, the non-speaking, the overlooked, as image-bearers and Spirit-bearers. I ask You to reveal Jesus through them in ways we have not seen before.

For my own family – I bless my loved ones as vessels of glory. I declare: You are not a mistake. You are not an afterthought. You are not less than. You are fearfully and wonderfully made. The Spirit of God rests upon you. Your life will teach us who God is.

Make Your Bride wide enough, deep enough, and humble enough to receive what You are pouring out on all flesh.

Challenge to the Reader

The Spirit has been poured out on all flesh – and the Bride is learning to recognize Him in unexpected vessels. But individual awakening and corporate inclusion must eventually become *architecture.* In the final chapter of this movement, everything converges: the garden that began in Genesis, the covenant that structured a people, the cross that opened access, and the crown that awaits a fully formed Bride. The Tree of Life itself becomes the sovereignty spine that holds the whole story together – from the garden humanity lost to the city the Bride becomes.

Scripture for Meditation

Joel 2:28–32 · Acts 2:14–21 · 1 Corinthians 12:12–27 · James 2:1–9 · Psalm 139:13–16

SIXTEEN

THE BRIDE ARCHITECTURE: FROM GARDEN TO CITY

This chapter pulls the whole book into one frame. From the first page of Scripture to the last, God has been building something — a people who carry His image, His covenant, His cross, and His crown. The Tree of Life stands quietly in the background of the story, then reappears in the foreground at the end. It is the sovereignty spine of the Bride.

Story Window — The Architect Who Saw the Whole Blueprint

Margaret had been designing buildings for thirty years. She was known for a philosophy that confused some clients but transformed every project: "I don't start with the rooms. I start with the spine — the load-bearing structure that everything else hangs on. If the spine is right, the building can carry anything."

When she came to faith in her fifties, she brought that same instinct to Scripture. She didn't read the Bible as a collection of inspirational passages. She read it as an architect reads a blueprint — looking for the load-bearing structure.

One night, she was reading Genesis and Revelation side by side. She placed her finger on Genesis 2 — the Tree of Life in the garden — and then on Revelation 22 — the Tree of Life in the city. Same tree. Different setting. Everything in between was the story of how access to that tree was lost, guarded, and finally restored.

She sketched a diagram on a napkin: a single vertical line — the Tree — with four horizontal crossbars marking the four movements of Scripture: Creation, Covenant, Cross, Crown. She stared at it and whispered, "That's the spine. Everything hangs on this."

Over the next year, she taught that diagram in her home group. She watched as business owners, teachers, parents, and young professionals began to see the Bible not as a scattered library but as a single architectural plan — a plan that ended not with destruction, but with a city where the Tree of Life feeds the nations and the Bride has become the dwelling place of God.

"The Bible," she told them, "begins with a garden and two people. It ends with a city and the nations. And the same Tree is at the center of both. God is not improvising. He is building."

What This Shows Us

The Bible is not a random collection of stories. It is the architectural blueprint for forming a people capable of carrying God's presence. That formation journey is what produces the Bride who becomes the city. The Tree of Life – running from Genesis to Revelation – is the sovereignty spine that holds the entire narrative together.

Scripture Deep Dive – The Tree Through the Story

In Eden, the Tree of Life stands at the center of the garden – a picture of unbroken union, a place where humanity can feed continually on God's own life, a reminder that life is received, not self-generated.

After the fall, the way to that Tree is guarded. Access is blocked – not to punish curiosity, but to prevent eternalizing a fallen state. The rest of Scripture becomes the story of how God reopens the way to that Tree without compromising His holiness.

By Revelation, the Tree of Life is back – on both sides of the river in the New Jerusalem, bearing fruit every month, its leaves for the healing of the nations. What was lost in a garden reappears in a city. The Bride herself has become that city.

The Four Movements – Creation, Covenant, Cross, Crown

The entire story – and this entire book – hangs on four words:

Creation – God's original design. Humanity is given identity and authority from union: "Let Us make man in Our image... and let them rule."

Covenant – God's binding relationship. He binds Himself to a people – Israel – to show what it looks like to walk with Him through history.

Cross – God's decisive intervention. He deals with sin, flesh, and every legal claim the enemy had, opening the way for New Creation humans.

Crown – God's shared rule with a formed Bride. A purified people share His reign in a renewed creation.

The Tree of Life runs through all four: Roots in Creation. Trunk in Covenant history. Axis where the Cross intersects time. Branches and canopy in the Crown – the city-Bride extending over the nations.

Formation Matrix – The Sovereignty Spine

Tree Element	Scripture Movement	Formation Meaning	Bride Application
Roots	Creation	Identity and authority given from union	"You were made in His image, to walk with Him"
Trunk	Covenant	Faithfulness, fear of the Lord, Ecclesia identity	"You learn covenant structure through history"
Axis	Cross	Flesh crucified; escape fantasies die; real authority anchored in blood	"Your old systems of self-rule end here"
Canopy	Crown	The Bride stands under fire, adorned, sharing His reign	"You carry His life to the nations"

When the spine is forgotten, sovereignty becomes self-assertion. When the spine is remembered, sovereignty becomes yielded strength – God's life flowing through a fully surrendered people.

The Maturation Pattern

Across the four movements, a repeated formation cycle emerges:

1. **Formation** – Identity given (Adam, Israel, the early Church)
2. **Covenant** – Relationship tested and deepened
3. **Failure** – Mixture, compromise, idolatry exposed

4. **Redemption** – God intervenes with mercy and discipline
5. **Sanctification** – Holiness restored, idols torn down
6. **Conflict** – Opposition arises as they carry true authority
7. **Adornment** – Purity, faithfulness, and love brought to maturity
8. **Union** – Shared glory, shared rule

This pattern plays out in Eden → Flood → Abraham → Exodus → Exile → Return. It plays out in Jesus' first coming → Cross → Church → Shaking → Final appearing. And it plays out in each believer's life, over and over, in smaller arcs. The Bride Architecture is simply this pattern applied to a people across time.

Formation Truth

The Bride's final posture – as described at the end of Revelation – is not confused, not divided, not mired in secret sins, not mocking God with lips while resisting Him with decisions. She has become: undivided in allegiance, clear in identity, clean in love, steady in holy fear, confident in the blood, bold in the Word, tender with the overlooked, rooted in union – not in anxiety. She is the architecture of God's own heart, visible. A Tree of Life people in a city of light.

For Leaders & Owners – Reflection Box

- If you steward a company, classroom, or team, your leadership seat is not *outside* the Bride Architecture – it is one of the branches through which the Tree of Life is meant to feed your generation.
- How you design culture, make decisions, and treat people is part of how the King prepares a city-Bride – not a separate secular side project.
- Where is your leadership rooted: in Creation identity (knowing whose image you bear)? In Covenant faithfulness? At the Cross (where self-rule died)? Under the Crown (where authority is shared, not seized)?

Formation Practices This Week

- **Inner** – *Walk the four movements.* This week, spend one day on each: Creation (Who did God design me to be?), Covenant

(Where am I learning faithfulness?), Cross (What self-ruled pattern must die?), Crown (What is God preparing me to carry?). Journal what the Spirit highlights.

- **Bodily** – *Stand under a tree.* Literally. Go outside, stand under a tree, and let it become a picture of the sovereignty spine. Roots reaching down. Trunk holding steady. Branches extending outward. Say: "Lord, make my life like this – rooted, steady, and fruitful."
- **Relational** – *Identify your branch.* Ask the Lord: "In the Bride Architecture, what branch am I? What part of the city am I being formed to carry?" Share your answer with one trusted person and ask them what they see.
- **Leadership** – *Build for the city.* Make one decision this week – in hiring, in culture, in generosity, in quality – that reflects the truth: "What I build is preparation for the King's city, not just this quarter's results."

Selah – Pause Here

Be still. The story that began in a garden with two people walking with God is heading toward a city filled with nations and the unfiltered presence of God. The Bride herself becomes that city. The Tree of Life stands at the center of both.

The question is not whether God is building. He has never stopped.

The question is whether you will let Him build *you* into what He has always intended – a living stone in the architecture of His heart.

Pray: *Jesus, You are the Alpha and the Omega, the Aleph and the Tav, the beginning and the end of my story and of history. You planted me in Your Creation. You pursued me in Covenant. You rescued me at the Cross. And You are preparing me for the Crown. I consent to all of it. Build me. Shape me. Place me where I belong in Your city. I am Yours.*

Activation – Final Sovereignty Declaration

I declare that the Tree of Life is my sovereignty spine. Life is from God, not from me. Authority flows from union, not independence. Fruit is the result of root and trunk, not effort alone.

My roots are in Creation – I was made in His image, to walk with Him. My trunk is in Covenant – I am learning faithfulness, fear of the Lord, and Ecclesia identity. My axis is at the Cross – my flesh is crucified, my escape fantasies are dead, and my real authority is anchored in His blood. My canopy is in the Crown – I stand under fire, adorned, sharing His reign.

I am not building my own tree. I am grafted into His.

The Spirit and the Bride say, Come.

Challenge to the Reader

The Bride Architecture has been revealed – from garden to city, from roots to canopy. But architecture without economics is theory. In the next movement of the book, the journey turns to what the Bride actually *does* with what she has been given. Stewardship is not a footnote to formation. It is the test that proves formation is real. The question shifts from "Who am I?" to "What have I been entrusted with – and how will I handle it before the King?"

Scripture for Meditation

Genesis 2:8–9 · Genesis 3:22–24 · Revelation 22:1–5 · Ephesians 2:19–22 · 1 Peter 2:4–5 · Revelation 21:1–5

SEVENTEEN

THE FORGOTTEN TRUTH: CHRIST IN YOU - THE UNSTOPPABLE LIFE

There is a sentence that sounds humble but quietly destroys authority. *I'm just a sinner saved by grace.* You have heard it in testimonies. You have said it yourself. It sounds safe. It sounds spiritual. It sounds like something no one could argue with. But if you let that sentence define you, it will strangle your capacity to pray with confidence, resist accusation, and walk in the purpose God designed before the foundation of the world.

Was there a time when it was true? Absolutely – you were a sinner, and you were rescued by grace so immense it rewrote your identity. But the New Testament does not keep calling you a sinner as your primary name. It calls you saint. New creation. Righteous in Christ. Child of God. Heir. Temple of the Holy Spirit. The early church understood this. They were deeply aware of grace and weakness. But they never used weakness as an identity label. They used it as the canvas for Christ's strength.

This chapter exists to recover a truth that the modern church has largely forgotten: the same Jesus who died for you rose to live *in* you. And the life He carries inside you is the same life that split tombs, stilled storms, and made religious systems tremble. You are not merely forgiven. You are inhabited.

Story Window – The Church That Forgot Who Lived Inside Them

Grace Community Church had all the markings of health. Weekly attendance was strong. The worship was sincere. The pastor was well-read, theologically trained, and genuinely kind. People loved being there.

But there was something missing that no one could quite name.

When someone in the congregation got sick, the response was always the same: "We'll pray for you," followed by a quick, almost apologetic prayer and a pivot to practical help – meal trains, medical referrals, hospital visits. All good things. But the idea that someone might actually lay hands on the sick and expect healing felt... uncomfortable. Not heretical. Just culturally unthinkable.

When a young man in the youth group began describing vivid dreams that seemed to carry spiritual weight, the youth pastor smiled politely and said, "That's interesting. Let's focus on what the Bible actually says." The dreams stopped being mentioned.

When a businesswoman in the church felt a stirring to confront an unjust situation in her industry – not with politics, but with prophetic clarity – she asked two elders for counsel. They affirmed her heart but cautioned, "Be careful. We don't want to be *those* kinds of Christians."

No one was hostile to the Holy Spirit. They simply did not expect Him to do much beyond comfort and conviction. Their theology said Christ lives in us. Their culture said, But let's not make a scene about it.

One Sunday, a visiting speaker – an older woman with no platform, no book deal, and no social media presence – stood up during a testimony time. She spoke quietly but with an authority that made the room still. She said: "I was in the early church movement in East Africa. We did not have buildings. We did not have seminaries. We had Jesus inside us, and that was enough. We prayed and the sick were healed. We spoke and chains broke. We were not special. We simply believed that when God said He would live in us, He meant it. I have traveled to many American churches. You are wonderful people. But I must tell you – many of you do not believe you carry what you carry."

The silence that followed was not offense. It was recognition. Something in the room cracked open – not the theology, which was already sound, but the *expectation,* which had been quietly suffocated by an unspoken agreement: *We believe the Bible, but we don't actually expect the Bible to happen through us.*

The following week, three separate people asked the pastor the same question: "Do we actually believe Christ lives in us – not as a metaphor, but as a fact that changes what's possible?"

The pastor didn't have a quick answer. He had a better one: "I think we need to find out."

What This Shows Us

Many churches hold correct theology about indwelling – Christ in you, the hope of glory – while functionally living as though His presence is decorative rather than operational. The gap is not doctrinal. It is experiential. And that gap explains why so many believers pray without confidence, lead without spiritual authority, and face accusation without the inner certainty that the One who conquered death is currently alive inside them.

Scripture Deep Dive – The Life That Cannot Be Stopped

The early believers did not see themselves as a weak group trying to survive history. They saw themselves as the Body of Christ on earth, sharing His life, His sufferings, and His authority.

Paul could say plainly: *"Christ lives in me"* (Galatians 2:20). *"You are the temple of the Holy Spirit"* (1 Corinthians 6:19). *"We are seated with Him in heavenly places"* (Ephesians 2:6). These are not metaphors. They are the backbone of New Covenant identity.

When Peter walked into a room with a crippled man, he did not pray, "Lord, if it be Your will, come down and do something." He said, *"What I have I give you. In the Name of Jesus Christ, rise and walk."* That sounds arrogant only if you forget who lives in you.

The Spirit in them was the same Spirit who raised Jesus from the dead. They were not waiting for reinforcement. They *were* the reinforcement. And the false humility that says "I'm just a sinner" would have been foreign to them – not because they were arrogant, but because they took the resurrection seriously.

Three layers of the forgotten truth:

- **Cleansing** – The blood of Jesus does not partially wash. It completely and continually cleanses. Your record of sin has been wiped out. He remembers your sins no more as a charge against you.

- **Access –** You enter the holiest place, not as a stranger, but as a child. The veil has been torn. The invitation is: *Come boldly to the throne of grace* (Hebrews 4:16). Boldness is not arrogance. It is trust in what the blood has done.
- **Authority –** You have been delivered from the power of darkness and transferred into the Kingdom of the Son He loves (Colossians 1:13). The enemy has no legal claim on you. His accusations cannot stick in the court of heaven when the blood is present.

Picture a courtroom. The accuser lists your failures. Every word may be factually accurate. Facts alone do not decide the case. The Judge looks at the evidence of the blood. The blood testifies: Debt paid. Sentence served. Righteousness granted. The gavel falls: *Justified.* The case is closed. The accuser has no further standing. When you agree with accusation after that, you are essentially reopening a case heaven has already dismissed.

Formation Matrix – From False Humility to Inhabited Authority

Old Identity Label	New Covenant Reality	Scripture Anchor
"I'm just a sinner"	"I am a new creation in Christ"	2 Corinthians 5:17
"I'm not worthy to pray boldly"	"I come by the blood, not by my mood"	Hebrews 4:16
"Holiness is beyond me"	"Christ in me is enough for this"	Colossians 1:27
"I should expect to fail"	"Greater is He who is in me"	1 John 4:4
."Who am I to expect God to move?"	"What I have, I give"	Acts 3:6

Formation Truth

The early church was not powerful because they were strong. They were powerful because they believed that the One who is strong had taken up permanent residence inside them. False humility sounds like worship, but it operates as unbelief – it agrees with the accuser's assessment instead of the King's verdict.

For Leaders and Owners – Reflection Box

> If you see yourself only as a sinner who happens to run a business, you will lead like a permanent liability. When you accept that Christ truly lives in you, you begin to walk shop floors, offices, and Zoom rooms as a carrier of divine life – not as a barely-tolerated extra in God's story.
>
> **Ask yourself this week:**

Formation Practices

- **Inner** – Retire false labels. Stop calling yourself what God no longer calls you. When "I'm just a sinner" surfaces, correct it: *I was a sinner. Now I am a new creation in Christ, saved by grace.*
- **Bodily** – Soak in identity Scriptures. Spend time in passages that define who you are now – new creation, righteousness, temple, beloved, heir. Read them as personal description, not abstract doctrine.
- **Relational** – Act like Christ actually lives in you. Ask: *If Jesus were standing physically where I am, how would He respond?* Then remember – He *is* in you. Begin to act accordingly in small, practical ways: praying for the sick, speaking comfort, confronting lies, refusing compromise.
- **Leadership** – Align your speech with your new nature. When you face a challenge, say, "Christ in me is enough for this." Not as a slogan, but as a statement of fact. Let that change how you address your team, your problems, and your prayers.

Selah – Pause Here

Sit quietly for sixty seconds. Ask the Holy Spirit: *Where have I been living as though You are a visitor instead of a resident? Where has false humility kept me from stepping into what You already deposited?* Do not rush past the answer.

Activation Prayer and Declaration

Speak this aloud:

Jesus, I thank You that You did not only die for me. You rose to live in me. I am not just a sinner saved by grace. I was a sinner. I am a new creation in Christ. Your Spirit dwells in me. Your life flows through me. Your authority rests on me.

I lay down false humility that calls You weak in me. I refuse to use my weakness as an excuse to bury what You have placed inside. I choose to speak in agreement with You: I have been crucified with Christ. It is no longer I who live, but Christ lives in me.

Let this forgotten truth become my daily reality – that I am Your Body on the earth, Your dwelling place, and Your vessel. Make me part of a Bride who knows who she is, so that, like the early Church, we cannot be stopped – not because we are strong, but because You are alive in us.

Challenge to the Reader

You have spent this chapter confronting the gap between what you believe about Christ's indwelling and how you actually live. But knowing the truth and thinking the truth are two different things. The mind is the battlefield where identity is either established or stolen. In the next chapter, we will lay out a practical, Scripture-based blueprint for how the mind is actually renewed – not through positive thinking, but through a complete operating-system upgrade from Adam's old code to Christ's new one. If the forgotten truth is *who* lives in you, the next chapter is about *how* that truth rewires the way you think, decide, and lead every single day.

Scripture for Meditation

Galatians 2:20 · 2 Corinthians 5:17 · Colossians 1:27 · 1 John 4:4 · Ephesians 2:6 · Acts 3:6 · Hebrews 4:16

EIGHTEEN

HOW TO RENEW YOUR MIND: A SCRIPTURE-BASED BLUEPRINT

Transformation does not begin with trying harder. It begins with thinking differently – from the inside out. Paul writes: *"Do not be conformed to this world, but be transformed by the renewing of your mind"* (Romans 12:2). Renewal is not positive thinking. It is not motivational self-talk. It is a shift from Adam's old operating system to Christ's new one.

Most people try to change behavior first. Scripture starts with identity. If you do not know who you are, every strategy for change will be built on sand. The previous chapter recovered the forgotten truth: Christ lives in you. This chapter asks: *Now how does that truth rewire the way you think?*

Story Window – The Executive Who Couldn't Stop the Loop

Renée was a VP of Operations at a mid-sized firm. She was competent, respected, and quietly miserable. Not because her job was bad – it was demanding but fair. Not because her faith was absent – she prayed every morning and attended a solid church. The problem was a loop inside her head that no amount of prayer seemed to break.

Every time she walked into a leadership meeting, the same internal script played: *You're going to say something wrong. They're going to figure out you don't belong here. You got lucky – this isn't really your level.*

She could quote identity Scriptures. She had journaled them, memorized them, even taught them in a women's Bible study. But the loop was louder than the verses. It ran beneath her awareness like background software, shaping her posture, her decisions, and the way she second-guessed everything.

One night, frustrated after a particularly draining meeting where she had stayed silent instead of offering an insight she knew was right, she sat with her Bible open and said aloud: "God, I know what You say about me. Why doesn't it stick?"

What followed was not a dramatic vision. It was a quiet realization. She had been trying to paste new truths on top of old agreements. She had never actually *identified* the agreements – the specific sentences running in the background – and deliberately revoked them.

That night she wrote them down, one by one: *You don't belong. You're not smart enough. You got here by accident. People are waiting for you to fail.* She stared at the list and realized something chilling: those were not her thoughts. They were her father's words, spoken over her at the dinner table for eighteen years, now running as internal code.

She crossed each one out. Beside each, she wrote what God's Word actually says: *You are chosen. You are seated with Christ. You have the mind of Christ. You are fearfully and wonderfully made.*

The loop did not disappear overnight. But for the first time, she had something she hadn't had before – awareness of what was playing, and a decision to change the station. Over weeks, then months, the new script began to take root. Her team noticed before she did. "You seem different in meetings," her COO said. "More settled. Like you're not fighting yourself anymore."

She wasn't. She had stopped trying to *improve* the old mind and started *renewing* it – replacing the operating system, not patching the bugs.

What This Shows Us

Mind renewal is not about willpower. It is about identification and replacement. Most believers try to think better without first discovering what they are thinking. The Scriptures call this taking every thought captive (2 Corinthians 10:5). You cannot take captive what you have not identified. Renewal begins with honest inventory, then deliberate agreement with what God says instead of what the old script says.

Scripture Deep Dive – The Blueprint for Renewal

Step 1 – Start with Who You Are, Not What You Do. "If anyone is in Christ, he is a new creation" (2 Corinthians 5:17). "You have put off the old self... and put on the new" (Ephesians 4:22-24). Renewal begins when you stop seeing yourself as *old you trying to improve* and start seeing yourself as *new creation learning how to live.* Ask yourself: When I think about myself, what identity is running in the background? Do I see myself more as broken trying to be fixed, or as new learning to walk? You will move in the direction of the identity you believe.

Step 2 – The Gate: Refusing to Be Conformed. Paul's command is not passive: "Do not be conformed to this world." The Greek word for conformed suggests being pressed into a mold. The world is constantly squeezing you into its shape – through media, culture, fear, comparison, and the opinions of people who do not know God's design for your life. Renewal requires a gate – a decision point where you say: *This thought does not align with Christ. I refuse it entry.*

Step 3 – The Word as Legal Document. When Jesus was tempted in the wilderness, He did not argue with the devil philosophically. He said: *"It is written."* Three times. That is not superstition. That is legal enforcement. Scripture is your inheritance document, signed in the blood of Jesus. When you put it in your mouth, you are not begging – you are bringing the will of God into view.

- *"By His stripes you were healed"* – you read that as a statement of your purchased healing.
- *"My God shall supply all your need"* – you read that as a direct, signed provision over your life.
- *"There is therefore now no condemnation"* – you read that as your legal verdict.

Step 4 – The Word as Mirror. James calls the Word a mirror. When you look into it, you see who you are in Christ. The enemy wants you to define yourself by past failure, current feeling, and visible limitation. The Word defines you by Christ's finished work, your union with Him, and heaven's verdict over your life. When accusation comes – *You are still that same person, you will never change, God is tired of you* – you answer with the Word: *"It is written: I am crucified with Christ; nevertheless I live, yet not I, but Christ lives in me"* (Galatians 2:20).

Formation Matrix – The Fact vs. Truth Grid

This grid, drawn from the raw notes, shows how Scripture repeatedly acknowledges facts while declaring a higher truth.

Situation	The Fact	The Truth Spoken
Sarah	Barren, past childbearing	"Is anything too hard for the Lord?" (Genesis 18:14)
Jairus' daughter	Dead	"She is not dead, but sleeping" (Mark 5:39)
The storm	Violent waves, real danger	"Peace, be still" (Mark 4:39)
Lazarus	Four days dead	"Come forth" (John 11:43)

Faith does not refuse facts. Faith refuses to let the fact become the final verdict. Facts report the situation. Faith reports the authority of God. Both can exist at the same time. But only one gets the final word.

Formation Truth

Renewal is not about ignoring reality – it is about submitting reality to a higher authority. The mind of Christ does not deny what is happening. It declares who has the last word. Scripture warns against two extremes: denial of reality (pretending something isn't happening) and agreement with defeat (letting the circumstance become your identity). Faith sits in the middle: *See clearly. Trust God fully. Speak carefully.*

For Leaders and Owners – Reflection Box

> For leaders and owners, mind renewal will confront how you think about money, power, risk, and people at work. The Spirit will challenge scarcity thinking, fear-based control, and burnout culture just as directly as He challenges lust or anger.

This week, ask:

Formation Practices

- **Inner** – Thought inventory with the Spirit. Take 20 minutes with a journal and write down the repetitive sentences in your mind – about yourself, your finances, your team, your future. Ask: *Which of these are lies I've agreed with?* Cross each one out and write a truthful replacement from Scripture.
- **Bodily** – 24-hour speech fast from negativity. Choose one full day where you will not speak self-insults, contempt toward others, or hopeless predictions. When you catch yourself starting, stop mid-sentence and replace it with a measured, truthful statement.
- **Relational** – Share your inventory with one trusted person. Tell them: "These are the loops I've been running. I'm replacing them with these truths. Hold me accountable."
- **Leadership** – In your next decision meeting, pause before reacting and ask: *Am I responding from the mind of Christ, or from the old script?* Let five seconds of silence become your gate.

Selah – Pause Here

Listen inwardly for the sentences you repeat about yourself – *I'm stupid, I always fail, I'll never change.* Notice how familiar they feel. Pray: *Lord, I renounce these agreements. Put Your words in my mouth about who I am, and teach me to agree with You.*

Activation Prayer and Declaration

Father, I come to You by the blood of Jesus. I bring my mind – not to improve it, but to renew it. I acknowledge that I have been running old scripts that do not agree with Your Word. Today I identify them. Today I revoke them. Today I replace them.

Where the enemy says "you'll never change," I declare: I am a new creation – old things have passed away. Where the world says "you're not enough," I declare: Christ in me is sufficient. Where my history says "this is who you are," I declare: I am who HE says I am.

Renew my mind, Lord. Not with positive thinking, but with the mind of Christ. Let me think as someone who has been crucified and raised. Let my thoughts align with the throne, not the tomb. In Jesus' Name.

Challenge to the Reader

You now have a blueprint for renewing your mind – not a theory, but a daily practice of identification, revocation, and replacement. But there is a question hovering over this entire journey that most believers have never had the courage to ask: *What if everything I was taught about the end of the story – about Revelation – is actually a formation journey and not a horror movie?* In the next chapter, we crack open the book that terrifies more Christians than any other and read it as what it actually is: a blueprint for the Bride's formation, not a schedule for her escape.

Scripture for Meditation

Romans 12:1–2 · 2 Corinthians 10:5 · Ephesians 4:22–24 · Philippians 4:8 · Isaiah 26:3 · Galatians 2:20 · 2 Corinthians 4:13

NINETEEN

REVELATION AS FORMATION BLUEPRINT: READING THE LAST BOOK AS TRAINING, NOT TERROR

There is a book in your Bible that most believers skip, and the ones who don't skip it usually read it with the wrong lens. The book of Revelation has been turned into a horror movie, a conspiracy timeline, a code to be cracked, or an escape map. Preachers have used it to sell fear. Novelists have used it to sell fiction. Entire denominations have built their identity around a specific interpretation of its sequence.

But what if Revelation is not primarily about *what will happen* to the world? What if it is about *what God is forming* in His people?

This chapter reads Revelation as a formation blueprint – a training manual for the Bride. Not because the events are unreal, but because the architecture is personal. Every stage of Revelation mirrors a stage of spiritual maturation. The Bride who reads this book correctly will not be terrified. She will be prepared.

Story Window – The Pastor Who Stopped Preaching Revelation

Pastor James had been a prophecy teacher for twenty years. He could draw timelines on a whiteboard that made every headline look like a Bible verse. His conference series on the end times filled auditoriums. People left his events both fascinated and frightened.

Then his daughter asked him a question he couldn't answer: "Dad, does Revelation make God look like He loves us, or like He's mostly angry?"

He opened his mouth to give the standard reply – God is just, judgment is necessary, we need to be ready – but the words felt hollow. He realized he had spent two decades teaching people to be afraid of a book that opens with Jesus walking among His churches, speaking words of correction *and* invitation, and closes with a wedding.

He took a sabbatical from prophecy preaching. He re-read Revelation slowly, not looking for timelines but for formation patterns. What he found changed everything. The letters to the churches were not threats – they were a spiritual diagnostic. The throne room was not distant – it was the lens through which every subsequent event should be interpreted. The judgments were not random – they were measured, progressive, and aimed at exposing what could not stand. The Bride at the end was not cowering – she was radiant, prepared, and saying *"Come."*

He came back to his church and said: "I've been reading Revelation as a schedule. It's actually a curriculum."

What This Shows Us

Revelation is the most misread book in the Bible, not because it is unclear, but because it has been read through the wrong framework. When read as formation – as a progressive journey from mixture to purity, from fear to faith, from compromise to crown – it becomes the most encouraging book in Scripture. The Bride does not escape Revelation. She is *formed by it.*

Scripture Deep Dive – The Formation Architecture of Revelation

1. The Prologue: You Meet Jesus as He Is (Revelation 1). Before any seal opens, before any trumpet sounds, John sees Jesus – glorified, sovereign, walking among His churches. Formation truth: you cannot interpret shaking rightly until you have seen the throne. Revelation does not start with fear. It starts with a vision of sovereignty and a Lamb who has already overcome.

2. The Seven Letters: He Searches and Corrects Your Heart (Revelation 2–3). Jesus addresses seven churches – each with a specific condition, a specific danger, and a specific promise. These are not ancient history. They are a spiritual diagnostic for every generation.

3. The Throne Room: You See His Sovereignty (Revelation 4–5). Before judgments fall, John sees worship and the Lamb at the center. The scroll of history is opened by the Lamb – the One who was slain. No angel, no human, no system can open it. Only sacrificial love has the authority to unfold history.

4. Seals, Trumpets, Bowls: Purification in Increasing Circles (Revelation 6–16). The scroll is opened by the Lamb. The pattern is measured — quarters, thirds, then fullness. Mercy is woven even into severity. These judgments expose the true nature of systems and hearts. Under pressure, repentance is either embraced or rejected. The Bride learns to see shaking not as God losing control, but as God refusing to let evil reign forever.

5. The Cosmic Conflict: Counterfeit Authority Exposed (Revelation 12–13, 17). A dragon, beasts, a false prophet, a harlot called Babylon. This section reveals the nature of counterfeit authority — systems that promise security, prosperity, and identity apart from God. The Bride learns to recognize what worship looks like when misdirected, what compromise sounds like when it whispers, *"Just bow a little – you can still love God in your heart."*

6. Harvest: Maturity Determines Outcome (Revelation 14). The Son of Man appears with a sharp sickle. The earth is ripe. Wheat and tares reach full maturity. Formation truth: the end is not arbitrary. People and systems ripen into what they have been cultivating. The Bride is called to mature in love, holiness, and loyalty — not in perfectionism, but in undividedness.

7. Fall of Babylon: Collapse of False Systems (Revelation 18). Merchants weep. Kings lament. Those who profited from her mourn her sudden collapse. Heaven rejoices. Babylon represents an economic-cultural-spiritual system built on exploitation, idolatry, and self-exaltation. No false empire, however sophisticated, will stand. The Bride cannot tie her hope to any Babylon, however comfortable it feels.

8. Marriage Supper: Purity Before Union (Revelation 19). "The marriage of the Lamb has come, and His Bride has made herself ready. She is granted to be clothed in fine linen, bright and clean — the righteous acts of the saints." The Bride is not passive. She *makes herself ready*, yet even that readiness is granted to her. Grace empowers preparation.

9. New Heavens, New Earth, New Jerusalem (Revelation 21–22). Heaven and earth are made new. The holy city comes down as a Bride prepared for her Husband. God declares: *"Behold, the dwelling of God is with humanity."* River of life. Tree of Life restored. No curse. Face-to-face presence. The Bride is not destined to float in a disembodied realm. She is destined to be a city-Bride, a people in whom God dwells, through whom He rules, in a renewed creation.

Formation Chart – The Seven Churches Grid

This grid preserves the full diagnostic from the manuscript drafts.

Church	Strength	Danger	Christ's Word	Formation Key	Promise to Overcomers
Ephesus	Doctrinal purity, endurance	Lost first love	"Remember... repent ... do the first works"	Return to intimacy	Eat from the Tree of Life
Smyrna	Faithful under persecution	Fear of suffering	"Do not fear... be faithful unto death"	Courageous endurance	Crown of life
Pergamum	Holding fast to Jesus' Name	Tolerating false teaching	"Repent, or I will fight against them"	Purging mixture	Hidden manna, white stone, new name
Thyatira	Love, service, growing works	Allowing Jezebel influence	"I gave her time to repent"	Zero tolerance for seduction	Authority over nations, morning star

Sardis	Reputation of life	Spiritual deadness beneath	"Remember... strengthen what remains"	Wakefulness and honesty	Clothed in white, name in Book of Life
Philadelphia	Little strength, true faithfulness	Pressure and opposition	"I have set before you an open door"	Hold fast what you have	Made a pillar in God's temple
Laodicea	Material wealth	Lukewarmness, self-satisfaction	"Buy from Me gold refined by fire"	Zealous repentance	Sit with Jesus on His throne

---

Formation Truth

Revelation is not just what will happen. It is how God finishes what He started – in the earth and in you. When you see your own formation mirrored in its architecture – letters that search your heart, a throne that anchors your faith, shakings that refine your loyalty, a wedding that crowns your preparation – you stop fearing the book. You start being formed by it.

For Leaders and Owners – Reflection Box

For anyone leading in business, education, or government, Revelation's Babylon is not just a distant symbol – it is a recognizable business model. You are called to discern where your industry disciples you into exploitation, image-driven success, or numbness to injustice, and to choose the Lamb's way instead – even when it costs you.

Ask yourself:

Formation Practices

- **Inner** – Read Revelation 2–3 slowly this week. Ask the Spirit: *Which church mirrors my current condition?* Let His words land as invitation, not threat.
- **Bodily** – Take one evening this week to sit in silence with Revelation 4–5. Do not analyze. Simply be in the throne room. Let your nervous system register that God is not anxious.
- **Relational** – Share one insight from the Seven Churches grid with a friend or spouse. Ask them: "Which church do you think I most resemble right now?"
- **Leadership** – Audit one business practice this week against the Babylon diagnostic: Does this practice exploit, manipulate, or build identity apart from God? If so, name it and begin correction.

Selah – Pause Here

Picture the throne room of Revelation 4. The One seated there is not pacing. He is not panicking. He is surrounded by worship. Now remember: the same God who sits on that throne lives inside you. Let that image settle your nervous system before you move forward.

Activation Prayer and Declaration

Jesus, You are the One revealed in this book. You walk among Your churches. You sit on the throne. You open the seals. You fight for truth. You cleanse, confront, and comfort.

Let this blueprint form me. Search me like You searched the seven churches. Show me the throne in every shaking. Teach me to recognize Babylon and refuse her seduction. Mature me as wheat, not tare. Make me part of a Bride who is not afraid of Revelation, but who reads it as a love story and a formation journey – moving from garden beginnings to city glory, from mixture to union, from compromise to crown.

Challenge to the Reader

You have now seen Revelation not as an escape hatch, but as a formation curriculum. The Bride who emerges from this book is not frightened – she is radiant. But there is a question the Spirit is raising in this generation that most churches have not yet answered: *When God said He would pour out His Spirit on ALL flesh, did He mean it?* In the next chapter, we will confront one of the most overlooked truths in the modern church – that the Spirit's outpouring includes vessels the Bride has been trained to ignore.

Scripture for Meditation

Revelation 1:17–18 · Revelation 2:7 · Revelation 4:2 · Revelation 19:7–8 · Revelation 21:1–4 · Revelation 22:1–2

TWENTY

THE SPIRIT POURED OUT ON ALL FLESH: THE OVERLOOKED VESSELS

When God said He would pour out His Spirit on *all flesh,* He meant exactly that. Not just on preachers. Not just on the eloquent. Not just on the socially seamless. All flesh. Sons and daughters. Old and young. Servants and those the world never puts on a stage. If the Bride only recognizes the polished, she will miss some of her most radiant members.

Story Window – The Boy Who Worshipped Without Words

The worship service was electric. Lights, sound, a band that could fill an arena. People raised their hands. Tears flowed. The presence of God was thick.

In the back row, a thirteen-year-old boy sat in a wheelchair. He did not speak – not because he chose not to, but because his neurology had never granted him that particular tool. He had autism. He communicated through a device on his lap, pressing images and symbols that formed sentences. Most Sundays, he pressed nothing during worship. He simply sat, eyes wide, body sometimes rocking gently, hands occasionally fluttering at his sides.

Some people assumed he didn't understand what was happening. Some felt sorry for him. A few shifted uncomfortably when his sounds – not words, but tones – rose above the music during a quiet moment.

His mother knew better. She had watched him at home during worship music. She had seen the tears. She had read the sentences he typed after services – sentences that carried more theological weight than most sermons: *"Jesus is close. I feel Him like water. He does not need my words. He already knows."*

One Sunday, the pastor did something unusual. He paused the service and said, "I believe the Lord wants to speak through someone who doesn't normally get the microphone." He walked to the back row, knelt beside the boy's wheelchair, and said, "Son, do you have something for us today?"

The boy's fingers moved slowly across his device. The room went silent. The speakers projected his typed words onto the screen:

"He is not far. He is here. Stop performing. Just be with Him. He came for all of us. Even the ones you don't think can carry Him."

No one moved. Several people wept — not out of pity, but out of conviction. A non-speaking boy had just preached the sermon of the year.

What This Shows Us

The Spirit's outpouring is not limited by human communication norms. God has always chosen unlikely vessels — Moses who stuttered, David who was overlooked, a virgin teenager who carried the Messiah. If the Bride narrows her definition of "Spirit-filled" to those who communicate the way we expect, she will amputate members that carry some of her deepest revelation.

Scripture Deep Dive — All Flesh Means All

"In the last days, I will pour out My Spirit on all flesh" (Acts 2:17).

We quote it. We celebrate it. But often, in practice, we narrow it. "All flesh" who communicate like us. "All flesh" who fit our expectations. "All flesh" who can perform spirituality in ways we're comfortable with.

But God's promise is larger than our categories. All flesh includes those who speak easily and those who cannot get words out. Those who process the world through typical neurology and those who experience it differently. Those the world puts on stages and those the world puts in back rows.

The Spirit does not require eloquence to inhabit a life. He requires yielding. And some of the most yielded hearts in the Body of Christ belong to people the church has not yet learned to hear.

This chapter is not about disability theology. It is about Bride theology. If the Bride is the corporate expression of Christ on earth – every member, every joint, every part – then excluding or overlooking members based on communication style or cognitive presentation is not just insensitive. It is architecturally incomplete. A city with missing foundations cannot stand.

Formation Matrix – Expanding the Bride's Recognition

What We Often Assume	What the Spirit Actually Does
Anointing looks eloquent	Anointing flows through yielded hearts regardless of speech
Worship requires musical ability	Worship is the posture of the spirit, not the performance of the voice
Prophecy requires articulate delivery	God spoke through a burning bush, a donkey, and stones ready to cry out
Leadership requires typical communication	Moses stuttered; God still sent him to Pharaoh
"All flesh" means "all functional adults"	"All flesh" means exactly what it says

---

Formation Truth

If the Bride only validates the polished, she reveals that she has confused performance with presence. The Kingdom has always been upside-down – the last are first, the weak carry strength, the foolish things confound the wise. A church that cannot receive from a non-speaking child has a smaller God than the one described in Scripture.

For Leaders and Owners – Reflection Box

Every leader carries this question into their organization: Who have I overlooked? Not because they lack capacity, but because their capacity doesn't fit my template?

In your business, your classroom, your team – who is the person you have not yet heard? Not the loudest voice, but the most faithful presence? The Spirit may be resting on them in ways you have not yet had eyes to see.

Practical step: This week, ask one person on your team who rarely speaks up: "What do you see that the rest of us might be missing?" Then listen without interrupting.

Formation Practices

- **Inner** – Ask the Holy Spirit: *Lord, have I limited who I believe You can speak through? Have I narrowed "all flesh" to "all flesh like me"?*
- **Bodily** – Attend to someone in your community who communicates differently. Sit with them. Do not fill the silence with your words. Simply be present and see what the Spirit reveals.
- **Relational** – Bless someone who has been overlooked. Not out of pity, but out of recognition. Say to them, directly: "I believe the Spirit of God rests on you. I want to learn from you."
- **Leadership** – Audit your church or organization's accessibility – not just ramps and elevators, but whether your culture actually makes space for people to contribute who don't fit the expected mold.

Selah – Pause Here

Think of someone you know – perhaps in your family, church, or workplace – who carries a quiet, steady presence with God but rarely gets recognized. Picture them before the Lord. Now hear the Spirit whisper: *That one carries Me too. Make room.*

Activation Prayer and Declaration

Father, You said ALL flesh. I repent for every time I narrowed that promise to fit my comfort. Open my eyes to the vessels I have overlooked – the quiet ones, the different ones, the ones the world does not celebrate.

For my own family – I bless my grandsons as vessels of glory. I declare: You are not a mistake. You are not an afterthought. You are not less than. You are fearfully and wonderfully made. The Spirit of God rests upon you. Your life will teach us who God is.

Make Your Bride wide enough, deep enough, and humble enough to receive what You are pouring out on all flesh.

Challenge to the Reader

You have just confronted the edges of the Bride's recognition – the places where she has been too narrow, too comfortable, too defined by human templates. But all of this – the identity recovered, the mind renewed, the Revelation blueprint understood, the overlooked vessels welcomed – leads somewhere. In the next chapter, we pull the entire book into one frame. From the first page of Scripture to the last, God has been building something: a people who carry His image, His covenant, His cross, and His crown. The Tree of Life stands quietly in the background of the story, then reappears in the foreground at the end. It is the sovereignty spine of the Bride. Turn the page. The architecture is about to come into full view.

Scripture for Meditation

Acts 2:17–18 · Joel 2:28–29 · 1 Corinthians 1:27–29 · 1 Corinthians 12:22–25 · Psalm 139:14

TWENTY-ONE

THE BRIDE ARCHITECTURE: FROM GARDEN TO CITY

This chapter pulls the whole book into one frame. From the first page of Scripture to the last, God has been building something – a people who carry His image, His covenant, His cross, and His crown. The Tree of Life stands quietly in the background of the story, then reappears in the foreground at the end. It is the sovereignty spine of the Bride.

Story Window – The Architect Who Found the Blueprint Was Always There

David had designed buildings for thirty years. Award-winning structures – libraries, hospitals, corporate headquarters. He understood that great architecture is never accidental. Every load-bearing wall, every window placement, every sight-line serves a purpose decided long before the first shovel breaks ground.

When he became a serious student of Scripture in his fifties, he began to notice something that thrilled him. The Bible was not a random collection of stories. It was an architectural document. Genesis laid foundations. Exodus built walls. The prophets were inspectors. Jesus was the cornerstone. And Revelation? Revelation was the final walkthrough – the moment the Architect shows the completed building.

"I've spent my career reading blueprints," he told his Bible study group one evening. "And I'm telling you – this Book has one. There is a single structural line running from Genesis 1 to Revelation 22, and it is not a metaphor. God is building a dwelling place for Himself out of living stones. The Tree of Life is the spine. Everything else hangs on it."

What This Shows Us

Scripture is not a random anthology. It is an architectural narrative. The same design that begins with a garden and a tree ends with a city and a restored tree. The Bride is the structure God has been building across the entire storyline — and the Tree of Life is her sovereignty spine.

Scripture Deep Dive — The Tree Through the Story

In Eden, the Tree of Life stands at the center of the garden. A picture of unbroken union. A place where humanity can feed continually on God's own life. A reminder that life is received, not self-generated.

After the fall, the way to that Tree is guarded. Access is blocked — not to punish curiosity, but to prevent eternalizing a fallen state. The rest of Scripture becomes the story of how God reopens the way to that Tree without compromising His holiness.

By Revelation, the Tree of Life is back — on both sides of the river in the New Jerusalem, bearing fruit every month, leaves for the healing of the nations. What was lost in a garden reappears in a city. The Bride herself has become that city.

Formation Chart — Creation · Covenant · Cross · Crown

The entire story — and this entire book — hangs on four words.

Movement	Meaning	Tree of Life Position	Bride's Formation
Creation	God's original design	Roots — the Tree is given	Identity established: image, breath, mandate
Covenant	God's binding relationship	Trunk — the Tree is guarded	Faithfulness learned: law, priesthood, testing

Cross	God's decisive intervention	Center Beam – the Tree becomes a Cross	Flesh crucified, access reopened, escape fantasies die
Crown	God's shared rule with a formed Bride	Branches & Canopy – the Tree is restored	Union, authority, shared reign in a renewed creation

Margin Verses:

- Roots: Genesis 1:26–28; Genesis 2:7; Genesis 2:8–9
- Trunk: Genesis 12:1–3; Exodus 19:4–6; Jeremiah 31:31–34
- Center Beam: Isaiah 53; John 19:30; Colossians 2:13–15
- Canopy: Romans 8:17–19; Revelation 19:7–8; Revelation 21:1–4; Revelation 22:1–2

The Sovereignty Spine

The Tree of Life is the sovereignty spine because it shows you:

- Life is from God, not from you.
- Authority flows from union, not independence.
- Fruit is the result of root and trunk, not effort alone.

Roots – Creation identity: You were made in His image, to walk with Him.
Trunk – Covenant structure: You learn faithfulness, fear of the Lord, Ecclesia identity.
Axis – Cross: Flesh is crucified. Escape fantasies die. Real authority is anchored in blood.
Canopy – Crown: The Bride stands under fire, adorned, sharing His reign.

When you forget the spine, you treat sovereignty as self-assertion. When you remember it, you treat sovereignty as yielded strength – God's life flowing through a fully surrendered people.

The Maturation Pattern

Across the four movements, a repeated pattern of formation emerges:

1. **Formation** – Identity given (Adam, Israel, the early Church)
2. **Covenant** – Relationship tested and deepened
3. **Failure** – Mixture, compromise, idolatry exposed
4. **Redemption** – God intervenes with mercy and discipline
5. **Sanctification** – Holiness restored, idols torn down
6. **Conflict** – Opposition arises as they carry true authority
7. **Adornment** – Purity, faithfulness, and love brought to maturity
8. **Union** – Shared glory, shared rule

This pattern plays out in Eden → Flood → Abraham → Exodus → Exile → Return. It plays out in Jesus' first coming → Cross → Church → Shaking → Final appearing. It plays out in your own life, over and over, in smaller arcs. The Bride Architecture is simply this pattern applied to a people across time.

Formation Truth

If you steward a company, classroom, or team, your leadership seat is not outside this Bride Architecture – it is one of the branches through which the Tree of Life is meant to feed your generation. How you design culture, make decisions, and treat people is part of how the King prepares a city-Bride, not a separate secular side project.

For Leaders and Owners – Reflection Box

Economics without rest becomes exploitation. Governance without rest becomes control. Authority without rest becomes abuse. The Tree of Life as sovereignty spine runs through both garden and city. The same Tree that feeds her in private is the Tree whose leaves heal nations in public.

Ask yourself: Is the way I run my organization more like a branch connected to the Tree of Life, or like a detached structure trying to produce fruit on its own?

Formation Practices

- **Inner** – Meditate on the Tree diagram. Ask: *Where am I on this Tree right now? Am I in the roots of fresh identity? The trunk of covenant testing? The axis of the Cross? Or the canopy of emerging authority?*
- **Bodily** – Take a walk this week and pray through each movement: Creation, Covenant, Cross, Crown. Let your body move as your spirit traces the story.
- **Relational** – Share the four-word framework with someone who needs perspective. Many believers feel lost in their story because they don't see the architecture. Help them locate themselves.
- **Leadership** – Evaluate one major decision you're facing this month. Run it through the sovereignty spine: *Is this decision rooted in identity (Creation)? Does it honor covenant (Covenant)? Has it been through the Cross (self-interest crucified)? Will it bear fruit for the Crown (Kingdom purposes)?*

Selah – Pause Here

Picture the Tree of Life – roots deep in Creation, trunk stretching through Covenant history, a horizontal beam where the Cross intersects, and a canopy reaching into glory. Now picture yourself standing inside that Tree. You are not outside the architecture. You are living in it. You always have been.

Activation Prayer and Declaration

Jesus, You are the Alpha and the Omega, the Aleph and the Tav, the beginning and the end of my story and of history. You planted me in Your Creation. You pursued me in Covenant. You rescued me at the Cross. And You are preparing me for the Crown.

I receive my place in Your Bride. I embrace my role in Your Ecclesia. I choose the Tree of Life over the knowledge of good and evil. I choose union over independence, obedience over appearance, and preparation over escape. Let my life, my family, my church, become part of this Bride Architecture – rooted in Your design, strengthened in Your covenant, crucified with You, and crowned only by Your hand. From Garden to City, You have been faithful. Be faithful to complete this work in me, and in us, until the day we see You face to face.

Challenge to the Reader

You have now seen the full architecture – from Garden to City, from Tree given to Tree restored. But there is a question that presses on every believer who sees this pattern: *If everything belongs to the King, then what does faithful management actually look like?* The next chapter will take you into one of the most misunderstood topics in the church – tithing, stewardship, and the radical shift from "What percentage do I owe?" to "Everything I have is His." The Bride is not only loved. She is entrusted.

Scripture for Meditation

Genesis 2:9 · Revelation 22:1-2 · Colossians 1:15-20 · Ephesians 2:19-22 · Revelation 21:1-4

TWENTY-TWO

THE STEWARDSHIP OF THE BRIDE: FROM PERCENTAGE TO BELONGING

There is a question many believers quietly carry but rarely say out loud: *Have we misunderstood tithing?* Not because they resist generosity. Not because they wish to give less. But because somewhere deep inside, something feels unfinished. The ten percent is paid. The box is checked. And yet the heart whispers: *Is this really all God meant?*

This chapter does not exist to abolish tithing or to minimize generosity. It exists to expand the conversation from a percentage to a posture – from calculating what is owed to recognizing what has been entrusted. Because the Bride of Christ is not being prepared for a wedding by measuring minimum requirements. She is being formed through relationship. Under law, a portion is sacred. Under love, everything becomes sacred.

Story Window – The Owner Who Gave Ten Percent and Kept the Rest for Himself

Marco was a generous man by any reasonable standard. He tithed consistently – ten percent of his company's profit went to his church every quarter. He supported missionaries, funded building projects, and gave to community causes. His name was on donor walls.

But Marco ran his business like it was entirely his own. Pricing decisions were made to maximize personal return. Employee wages were kept at market minimum. Vendor relationships were leveraged for every possible advantage. When a supplier went through a crisis and asked for extended terms, Marco's answer was quick: "That's not my problem. Business is business."

One day, a mentor who had known him for decades asked a question that made Marco uncomfortable: "Marco, you tithe your income. But do you steward your business?"

"What do you mean? I run a profitable company."

"I mean — do you run it like it belongs to God, or like it belongs to you with a ten percent tax for God?"

The question landed hard. Marco realized that his generosity had become a boundary: ten percent was sacred; ninety percent was his. He had compartmentalized his life — a spiritual portion and a secular portion — and the secular portion operated on entirely different values.

Over the following year, Marco began to ask different questions. Not "How much do I give?" but "How faithfully am I managing what God has entrusted to me?" That question touched wages, vendor relationships, hiring practices, pricing integrity, and the culture he was building. Giving didn't decrease. But the scope of stewardship expanded to include everything.

What This Shows Us

Tithing can become the finish line of obedience — the place where the spiritual obligation ends and the "real life" begins. But the New Covenant does not divide life into sacred and secular. It invites the Bride to see everything as part of God's household. The shift is not about giving less. It is about surrendering more.

Scripture Deep Dive – From Levitical Portion to Royal Priesthood

Under the Mosaic covenant, tithes sustained the Levitical priesthood. The tribe of Levi had no land inheritance, so the people of Israel supported them through the tithe. The Temple required provision, and the system required structure.

But Jesus did not come merely to reform that system. He fulfilled it. When Christ rose as our High Priest forever, the structure surrounding the priesthood changed. There is no longer a Temple tax. There is no Levitical tribe receiving offerings. There is no national covenant economy tied to agricultural land.

Instead, the New Testament reveals something astonishing: the people themselves become the temple. And those same people are called a royal priesthood (1 Peter 2:9). This means the flow of responsibility shifts. In the old covenant, the people supported the priests. In the new covenant, the people themselves are the priests who serve under Christ their High Priest. And priests are not defined merely by what they give. They are defined by what they steward.

Paul writes: *"Present your bodies as a living sacrifice, holy and acceptable to God"* (Romans 12:1). Under the old system, sacrifices involved grain, oil, and animals. Under the new covenant, the offering becomes us. Our lives. Our choices. Our resources. Our influence. The Bride does not tithe her affection. She offers herself completely.

The formation hidden in the Old Testament law was broader than simple financial support. Three distinct tithes served three purposes: provision sustained the priesthood, celebration honored the goodness of God, and care extended toward the vulnerable. These rhythms cultivated a culture of provision, presence, and justice. The Bride learns these same rhythms today – not through legal requirement, but through spiritual maturity.

Formation Matrix – Tithing vs. Stewardship

Dimension	Tithing Mindset	Stewardship Mindset
Core Question	"What is required of me?"	"What reflects the heart of my King?"
Measurement	Obedience in percentages	Faithfulness in fruit
Scope	A defined portion is sacred	Everything is sacred
Identity	Contributor to sacred work	Participant in sacred work
Outcome	Discipline the heart	Transform the heart
Bride Preparation	Calculate minimum requirements	Surrender everything to the King

---

Formation Truth

The difference between tithing and stewardship can be summarized in two questions. Tithing asks: *What is required of me?* Stewardship asks: *What reflects the heart of my King?* A percentage can be measured. Belonging cannot. And belonging is what forms the Bride.

For Leaders and Owners – Reflection Box

> When believers begin to consider that everything belongs to God, an honest question sometimes arises: *What if He asks for more than I expected?* But the gospel answers that question before it even finishes forming. Christ did not give ten percent of Himself. He gave everything.
>
> **Pause for a moment. Sit with the Lord quietly. Not with calculations. With honesty. Consider what stewardship would look like if it were not merely an obligation, but an act of preparation.** Because one day we will stand before Christ. And the question will not be whether we reached a certain percentage. The question will be whether we were faithful with what He entrusted to us. Faithfulness is the evidence of relationship. And relationship is what forms the Bride.

Formation Practices

- **Inner** – Ask the Holy Spirit: *Where have I drawn a line between what's Yours and what's mine? Where does my stewardship stop and my self-interest begin?*
- **Bodily** – Review one financial decision you made this month – not for guilt, but for alignment. Did it reflect the heart of the King, or the logic of the marketplace alone?
- **Relational** – Have an honest conversation with your spouse or a trusted friend about finances. Not about budgets, but about posture: *Are we managing God's resources or protecting our own?*

- **Leadership** – Audit one area of your business this week through stewardship eyes: wages, vendor relationships, or pricing. Ask: *If Jesus reviewed this, would He see faithfulness or self-interest?*

Selah – Pause Here

Read Revelation 19:7–8 slowly: *"The marriage of the Lamb has come, and His Bride has made herself ready. She was granted to be clothed in fine linen, bright and pure – for the fine linen is the righteous acts of the saints."* Notice what prepares the Bride. Not financial quotas. Not institutional obligations. Righteous acts. A life aligned with the character of the King.

Activation Prayer and Declaration

Father, I confess that I have sometimes treated stewardship as an obligation instead of a privilege. I have drawn lines between what is Yours and what I considered mine. Today I erase those lines.

Everything I have – my income, my business, my time, my influence, my growth – belongs to You. I am not an owner. I am a steward. Teach me to manage what You have entrusted with the same faithfulness You showed when You entrusted Your Son for my redemption.

Let my stewardship prepare me for the wedding. Let my faithfulness become the linen I wear before Your throne. I am Yours – not ten percent of me, but all of me. In Jesus' Name.

Challenge to the Reader

Stewardship is not the final stage of formation. It is the threshold. When the Bride learns to manage what belongs to the King, she becomes trustworthy with greater responsibility. In the next and final chapter, we will explore how stewardship grows into authority – how a people prepared through faithfulness begin to participate in the governance of the

Kingdom. Because the Bride is not only loved. She is entrusted. And entrusted people are given power.

Scripture for Meditation

Genesis 14 · Psalm 110 · Hebrews 7 · Romans 12:1 · 1 Peter 2:9 · Revelation 19:7–8

TWENTY-THREE

THE AUTHORITY OF THE BRIDE: FROM STEWARDSHIP TO GOVERNANCE

Stewardship is where formation begins. But it is not where formation ends. Faithfulness prepares the heart, yet Scripture reveals that God's intention has always extended beyond faithful management. The purpose of stewardship is not simply responsibility – it is preparation for authority.

From the beginning, God created humanity not only to receive His provision but to participate in His governance. Dominion was the original assignment. We were not designed merely to survive within creation. We were entrusted to steward it, cultivate it, and govern it under God's direction. The garden was not simply a place of beauty – it was a training ground for governance.

This is the final chapter of Book 4. Everything you have walked through – the Aleph-Tav blueprint, Enoch and Job, the King's garden, the Ezer revelation, the blood, the Word, the sovereignty declaration, Revelation as formation, the overlooked vessels, the Tree of Life sovereignty spine, and stewardship as belonging – has been leading here. The Bride has been formed. Now she steps into her assignment: shared rule with the King.

Story Window – The Woman Who Was Given the Keys

For fifteen years, Miriam managed a regional nonprofit that served at-risk youth. She was faithful – meticulously faithful. Every grant was accounted for. Every report was on time. Every dollar stretched further than anyone thought possible. Auditors loved her. Board members trusted her. She was the definition of a faithful steward.

Then the founder retired and, to everyone's surprise, handed the organization to Miriam. Not management – *ownership.* Full authority. Full responsibility. Full governance.

Miriam's first response was panic. "I know how to manage," she told a mentor. "I don't know how to lead."

Her mentor smiled. "That's exactly why he chose you. The ones who know how to manage without grasping are the ones who can be trusted with authority."

The transition was not smooth. Decisions that used to require approval now required her discernment. Problems that used to be someone else's responsibility were now hers. She had to hire, fire, cast vision, and make calls that would affect families for years. The weight was different from management. Management handles what exists. Authority shapes what comes next.

But something she had built during fifteen years of stewardship now served her: she knew how to listen. She knew how to be quiet before God and wait for direction. She knew how to hold resources without grasping them. She knew how to make decisions that honored people, not just metrics.

Three years later, the organization had doubled its impact. Not because Miriam was louder or more aggressive than the founder. But because she governed the way she had stewarded – with open hands, attentive ears, and an unshakable conviction that everything in her care ultimately belonged to Someone else.

What This Shows Us

Authority is not the opposite of stewardship – it is its fulfillment. The Bride is not promoted from servant to ruler. She discovers that faithful service *was* ruler training all along. Jesus said it plainly: "You were faithful over a few things. I will make you ruler over many things" (Matthew 25:21).

Scripture Deep Dive – The Original Mandate Restored

Before there was a temple, before there was a priesthood, before there was even a nation of Israel, God spoke a mandate over humanity: *"Let us make mankind in our image, according to our likeness, and let them have dominion"* (Genesis 1:26).

The fall did not erase humanity's calling, but it distorted humanity's relationship with authority. Instead of governing under God's direction, humanity attempted to define good and evil independently. Authority separated from obedience always leads to corruption.

When Jesus begins His ministry, His central message is not merely forgiveness. It is the arrival of a kingdom: *"Repent, for the kingdom of heaven is at hand."* Jesus did not come only to rescue individuals. He came to restore the reign of God within humanity. Redemption is more than forgiveness. It is a change of jurisdiction.

The five refining separations of Matthew 24–25 reveal the formation process that prepares a people for this authority:

Refining Separation	**What Is Tested**	**Formation Dimension**
Faithful vs. Unfaithful Servant (24:45–51)	Loyalty in hidden responsibility	Integrity when no one watches
Ten Virgins (25:1–13)	Preparedness and sustained readiness	Oil cannot be borrowed – personal intimacy
Talents (25:14–30)	Stewardship of entrusted resources	Courage to multiply, not hide
Sheep and Goats (25:31–46)	Embodied compassion	The King's nature flowing through His people
Life of the Age (25:46)	Final alignment	Participation in the coming Kingdom

Jesus is not merely warning about judgment. He is revealing the formation process through which a people become ready for shared governance.

Each refining separation exposes a deeper layer — from loyalty to watchfulness to stewardship to embodied love to ultimate alignment.

Formation Chart – The Bride Formation Wheel

This diagram, developed throughout the raw notes, represents the Crown Jewel Visual of the entire Kingdom Economics series. The Bride Formation Wheel shows transformation from believer → Bride → City happening through five access movements that activate twelve internal foundations.

The Five Access Movements (from John 13–17):

Movement	Interior Formation	Scripture Doorway
Cleansing	Humility and surrender	John 13
Abiding	Union and life-flow	John 15
Authority	Prayer and priesthood	John 16
Unity	Corporate alignment	John 17
Glory	Habitation and radiance	Revelation 21

The Twelve Foundations Within the Wheel:

Foundation	Formation Within the Bride	Tribe Echo	Governance Expression
1 – Identity	Image-bearing restored	Reuben	Self-governance
2 – Covenant	Loyalty to God	Simeon	Covenant faithfulness
3 – Wisdom	Discernment	Levi	Instruction
4 – Stewardship	Economic order	Judah	Leadership

5 – Authority	Spiritual authority	Dan	Justice
6 – Provision	Trust in God's supply	Naphtali	Distribution
7 – Alignment	Obedience to God's order	Gad	Strategy
8 – Fruitfulness	Life multiplication	Asher	Prosperity
9 – Endurance	Faith through testing	Issachar	Timing
10 – Vision	Prophetic sight	Zebulun	Expansion
11 – Unity	Covenant community	Joseph	Reconciliation
12 – Glory	Divine habitation	Benjamin	Presence

At the center of the Wheel is Christ Himself. Everything flows from union with Him outward. The believer stands in Christ at the center, and formation radiates through the five access movements, which activate the twelve foundations. The reader is not studying architecture. They are entering it.

The Bride's Final Posture

By the end of Revelation – and by the end of this book – the Bride is no longer:

- Confused about escape vs. arrival
- Divided between Gnostic fantasy and embodied calling
- Mired in secret sins that bleed out the anointing
- Mocking God with lips while resisting Him with decisions

She has become:

- Undivided in allegiance

- Clear in identity
- Clean in love
- Steady in holy fear
- Confident in the blood
- Bold in the Word
- Tender with the overlooked
- Rooted in union, not in anxiety

She is the architecture of God's own heart, visible. A Tree of Life people in a city of light. The Spirit and the Bride say, *"Come."*

Formation Truth

The purpose of this entire book has been one thing: to form a people who can carry authority without collapse. Every chapter has been building load-bearing walls inside you – identity, rest, purity, courage, mind renewal, Scripture mastery, holy fear, and stewardship. Authority is the crown placed on a prepared head. Without the formation, authority becomes abuse. With it, authority becomes service – the Bride governing alongside her King.

For Leaders and Owners – Reflection Box

> The original mandate was never revoked. You were created to govern – not to dominate, but to administer God's order in your sphere. Your business is a training ground for eternal governance. Your leadership decisions are rehearsals for shared rule.
>
> **Final audit:** Look at the way you carry authority. Does it reflect the Lamb – who leads by sacrifice, governs by love, and holds power with open hands? Or does it reflect the beast – who seizes, manipulates, and controls?
>
> The Bride governs like the Lamb. That is the authority this book has been building toward.

Formation Practices

- **Inner** – Ask the Lord: *Where have You been preparing me for authority that I have not yet stepped into – not because it wasn't available, but because I didn't believe I was ready?*
- **Bodily** – Physically write out Matthew 25:21: *"Well done, good and faithful servant. You were faithful over a few things; I will make you ruler over many."* Place it where you will see it every morning this week.
- **Relational** – Identify one area where God is asking you to step from management into governance – in your family, your business, your community. Tell one trusted person: "I believe God is expanding my assignment. Will you walk with me?"
- **Leadership** – Make one governance decision this week that reflects the Lamb's way instead of the world's way – even if it costs you. Let that decision become the first fruit of the authority this book has been forming in you.

Selah – Final Pause

Close your eyes. Picture the New Jerusalem – twelve gates open, twelve foundations gleaming, the river of life flowing, the Tree of Life bearing fruit for the healing of nations. Now hear the voice of the King: *"Come, I will show you the Bride."* And what John sees is not a person. It is a city. A people. An architecture of love and authority.

You are part of that city. You have always been part of that city. This book has simply been showing you the blueprint that was there before the foundation of the world.

Final Sovereignty Declaration

Let this close the book in your own mouth:

Jesus, You are the Alpha and the Omega, the Aleph and the Tav, the beginning and the end of my story and of history. You planted me in

Your Creation. You pursued me in Covenant. You rescued me at the Cross. And You are preparing me for the Crown.

I receive my place in Your Bride. I embrace my role in Your Ecclesia. I choose the Tree of Life over the knowledge of good and evil. I choose union over independence, obedience over appearance, and preparation over escape.

Let my life, my family, my church, become part of this Bride Architecture – rooted in Your design, strengthened in Your covenant, crucified with You, and crowned only by Your hand.

From Garden to City, You have been faithful. Be faithful to complete this work in me, and in us, until the day we see You face to face.

The Spirit and the Bride say: Come.

Amen.

Challenge to the Reader – A Final Word

You have walked the entire formation journey of Book 4. From the Aleph-Tav blueprint hidden in the first verse of Scripture, through the wilderness of Enoch and Job, into the King's secret garden, past the Ezer revelation and the dismantling of mockery, through the blood and the Word and the renewed mind, across the Revelation blueprint and the overlooked vessels, down the sovereignty spine of the Tree of Life, through stewardship, and now into authority.

You are not the same person who opened this book.

But the journey does not end here. Book 5 awaits – where the Bride who has been formed is now *measured.* The twelve foundations are revealed. The city is inspected. The governance architecture appears. And the wheels within the wheel – personal awakening, corporate formation, Kingdom architecture – begin to turn together under the direction of His Spirit.

Before God builds His city, He awakens His people. You have been awakened.

Now step through the doorway.

Scripture for Meditation

Genesis 1:26–28 · Matthew 25:21 · John 13–17 · Revelation 19:7–8 · Revelation 21:1–4 · Revelation 22:1–2 · Revelation 22:17

APPENDIX A: THE 12 DOORWAYS OF FORMATION

APPENDIX A: The Twelve Doorways of Formation – The Hebrew Calendar as the Bride's Journey

The Hebrew calendar is not simply a record of ancient observances. It is a formation cycle. Each month becomes a doorway through which the Bride is shaped.

Month	Doorway	Formation Theme
1. Nissan	Redemption	Passover – identity shifts from slavery to covenant belonging. "Will you leave Egypt behind?"
2. Iyar	Healing and Provision	God as Jehovah Rapha – wounds surface, old patterns break, trust grows
3. Sivan	Covenant	Torah at Sinai – freedom is not lawlessness but alignment with God's nature
4. Tammuz	Testing	Golden calf tension – the Bride decides whether to remain faithful when God seems distant
5. Av	Brokenness	Temple destruction – false structures collapse so God can build something eternal
6. Elul	Return	"The King is in the field" – repentance, preparation, responding to the nearness of the King
7. Tishrei	The King	Trumpets, Atonement, Tabernacles – holiness, mercy, and dwelling presence
8. Cheshvan	Hidden Faithfulness	No major feast – faith matures in the quiet months

9. Kislev	Light in Darkness	Hanukkah – perseverance; faithfulness preserves the flame
10. Tevet	Refinement	Siege and hardship – gold is purified through fire
11. Shevat	Renewal	New Year of the Trees – unseen life awakens beneath the soil; roots deepen before branches expand
12. Adar	Reversal	Esther – God turns plans of the enemy into instruments of deliverance. Repositioning occurs. Authority shifts.

After Adar comes Nissan. The cycle restarts with redemption. But the people entering this new Nissan are not the same people who began the previous year. They have been formed. Prepared. Refined. And now they are ready to step forward into a new season with deeper understanding of the One who sits upon the throne – the One who is forever proclaimed in heaven as Holy, Holy, Holy.

APPENDIX B: ARAMAIC AND HEBREW TERMS

APPENDIX B: Aramaic and Hebrew Terms Used in This Book

Term	Language	Meaning / Usage in This Book
Aleph-Tav (את)	Hebrew	First and last letters of the Hebrew alphabet; God's signature in Genesis 1:1; Jesus as "the Beginning and the End"
Ezer (עֵזֶר)	Hebrew	Helper/Rescuer – used 21 times in the OT, 16 times of God Himself; the Bride's true identity
Halak et ha'Elohim	Hebrew	"He walked with God" – describing Enoch's shared-life communion (Genesis 5:24)
Et (את)	Hebrew	Untranslatable grammatical marker carrying the Aleph-Tav signature
Shalom (שָׁלוֹם)	Hebrew	Wholeness, completeness, integrated being – nothing missing, nothing broken
Oikonomia (οἰκονομία)	Greek	Household management – root of "economy"; stewardship of God's resources
Thlipsis (θλῖψις)	Greek	Tribulation – literally pressure, compression, squeezing
Apantesis (ἀπάντησις)	Greek	"To meet" – civic delegation greeting a visiting king; used in 1 Thessalonians 4 for the royal arrival
Kolasis (κόλασις)	Greek	Corrective judgment that restrains or removes what is harmful

Dekatē (δεκάτη)	Greek	A tenth – the NT word for tithe; a mathematical portion, not a concept
Ma'aser (מַעֲשֵׂר)	Hebrew	A tenth – the OT word for tithe; literally one-tenth of something
Ecclesia (ἐκκλησία)	Greek	Called-out assembly – not a building but a governing council of believers
Yeshua HaMashiach	Hebrew/Aramaic	Jesus the Messiah – the full covenant name
Selah (סֶלָה)	Hebrew	Pause, reflect, weigh – used throughout the Psalms and in this book as formation pauses
Purim	Hebrew	Festival celebrating divine reversal from the Book of Esther
Adar	Hebrew	12th month of the Hebrew calendar – the doorway of reversal and repositioning
Nissan	Hebrew	1st month of the Hebrew spiritual year – the doorway of redemption (Passover)
Jubilee (Yovel)	Hebrew	50th year – debts cancelled, land returned, slaves released; the reset of society

APPENDIX C: ARAMAIC FORMATION GLOSSARY

Appendix C – Aramaic Formation Glossary

Term	Meaning
Ḥoba	Unfinished alignment – missing the mark, inviting correction and return rather than condemnation
Shbaq / Shubqana	Release, unbinding – forgiving, loosening claims, letting go so God can heal
Haymanuta	Trust formed through experience – confidence born from walking with God
Ṭuva	Life-aligned goodness – wholeness and beauty when aligned with God's ways
Nishmatha	The breath of life – the God-given in-breath animating spirit, soul, and body
Rukha	Spirit, wind, breath in motion – the dynamic presence of God
Abwoon	Source-Father – the intimate, origin-giving God who births and sustains

APPENDIX D: ESCAPE VS. ROYAL ARRIVAL

Appendix D – Escape vs. Royal Arrival: Two-Column Contrast Grid

Dimension	Escape Framework	Royal Arrival Framework
Earth's destiny	Doomed stage to be abandoned	Destined for renewal under Christ's reign
Believer's role	Survive and hold on until evacuation	Prepare, steward, and overcome
Meaning of "caught up"	Secret removal to avoid hardship	Public welcome of the returning King
"As in the Days of Noah"	Escaping the flood	Righteous preserved through shaking
View of tribulation	Something to escape	Training ground and purifying fire
Identity of the Church	Fragile remnant surviving until extraction	Prepared Bride carrying glory
Motivation for holiness	Fear of being left behind	Desire to be a pure Bride for the King
How headlines are read	Countdown clock to disappearance	Birth pangs of the Kingdom's fullness
View of resurrection	Minimized	Central – gateway into shared rule

APPENDIX E: THE DOCTRINE OF THE TONGUE

The Doctrine *of the* Tongue:
Heart, Speech & Wholeness

HEART (*Lev / Kardia*)
Source of Belief & Desire

INTERNAL ABUNDANCE
Overflow of the Heart

TONGUE (*Lashon / Glôssa*)
Instrument of Release

Power of the Tongue

LIFE
Healing · Peace · Strength

WHOLE
BODY & SOUL
Aligned with God's Design

DEATH
Corrosion · Anxiety · Decay

DRY BONES
& TROUBLED SPIRIT
Fragmented & Broken

RESTORATION & WHOLENESS

FRAGMENTATION & HARM

BONUS: SIMPLIFY SYSTEM: THE W.E.A.L.T.H. SYSTEM

SIMPLIFY SYSTEM

Sovereignty Requires Structure

Book 3 formed you.

It confronted identity.
It stripped false coverings.
It aligned you with covenant.

Now structure must follow.

Because revelation without architecture collapses.

Sovereignty must produce systems.

The Shift

Wealth is not first financial.

It is structural.

Identity precedes influence.
Governance precedes growth.
Order precedes increase.

Simplify System exists to translate identity into infrastructure.

What It Is

Simplify System is governance before growth.

Clarity before cash flow.
Covenant before contracts.
Structure before scale.

It equips you with:

- Executable Kingdom-aligned strategy
- Operational frameworks that withstand scrutiny
- Revenue models built on integrity
- Leadership systems grounded in maturity
- Scalable structure without compromise

This is disciplined construction.

The W.E.A.L.T.H. Framework

W.E.A.L.T.H. establishes order:

W – Wisdom before movement
E – Execution with alignment
A – Architecture over ambition
L – Leadership through governance
T – Timing without striving
H – Harvest that honors Heaven

When order is established, increase stabilizes.

The 7 Jars

The 7 Jars introduce covenant-based stewardship.

They define containers for flow.

They establish:

- Protection
- Allocation
- Multiplication
- Preservation
- Release

Without containers, increase leaks.
With governance, wealth matures.

Declaration

I build from identity, not insecurity.
I build from governance, not impulse.
I build from covenant, not competition.

My systems reflect order.
My revenue reflects integrity.
My leadership reflects maturity.

What I build will endure.

Now I construct.

SIMPLIFY SYSTEM

Sovereignty. Structure. Scale.

Begin the architecture: **simplifysystems.net**

ABOUT THE AUTHOR

"Do you want to go on an adventure with Me?"

That question redirected my life.

At 20 years old, after years of working retail and moving through school on autopilot, I asked God, "Is this all there is?"

The answer came clearly: "Join the Navy."

It made no logical sense. I had no military background. No technical experience. No plan. But I said yes.

That yes launched a nearly three-decade career inside some of the most complex and high-security environments in the world.

I began in the U.S. Navy, where I was placed into advanced technology systems I had never touched before—and mastered them.

From there, I worked inside major financial institutions including Chase (BankOne) and Bank of America, leading enterprise architecture, SOX compliance initiatives, vulnerability management systems, and DMZ security infrastructure.

While architecting Bank of America's perimeter security, I identified foundational vulnerabilities within Microsoft's Windows 2000 operating system. Where others said it could not be hardened to enterprise-grade standards, I engineered the solution that became Microsoft's first hardened server implementation.

My career has followed one consistent pattern: When others say it cannot be done, I build it.

Over the years, I have:

- Designed hardened enterprise operating systems
- Architected secure banking infrastructure protecting billions
- Led Six Sigma and compliance teams
- Built vulnerability management systems
- Repaired failed infrastructures
- Transformed chaotic environments into governed systems

But the deeper pattern has always been this: I partner with the genius of God. I do not see "impossible" as a barrier. I see it as an invitation.

In 2008, I founded Cyber Secure Online to bring enterprise-level cybersecurity and systems architecture to small and mid-sized organizations who were told they were "too small" for serious protection.

Later, I built Simplify System – an integrated framework combining sales, CRM, marketing, ecommerce, productivity, and enterprise-grade cybersecurity into one unified architecture for sovereign builders.

My work is not motivational. It is structural.

I help leaders build systems that endure scrutiny, scale with integrity, and reflect governance – not chaos.

Kingdom Economics was written to provide the blueprint. Simplify System exists to provide the architecture.

After 30 years of enterprise systems engineering, cybersecurity architecture, and governance leadership, one truth remains constant:

God is a genius. My role is to say yes and build what He reveals. And I still fix impossible things.

–

Dianne Beattie
U.S. Navy Veteran
Enterprise Systems Architect
Founder, Simplify System & Cyber Secure Online
Kingdom Business Strategist

Establish Your Legacy of Faith for the Generations

Our Family
DECREE OF BLESSING & HOPE

Our Family Decree of Blessing & Hope is an invitation to begin building Your Legacy of faith through decreeing His word over you and your family to be passed down until Jesus comes back in all His glory!

WHY
decreeing matters. It's a discipline to develop, allowing us to pray without ceasing,

HOW
decreeing works. We agree, receive, declare, record, and sign what God has already spoken to you.

WHAT
decreeing produces... What we decree is established forever and His light shines on our ways.

- Prayer that removes your motives and surrenders to God's Word.
- Partnership with the Holy Spirit in shaping your family's destiny
- A foundation that anchors every generation in God's unchanging truth and gives your descendants a record to return to in every season of life.

FamilyDecree.org

LIVING SUPERNATURALLY MENTORING

How to Live and Operate in the Supernatural

Step into a mentoring relationship that activates:

The Five keys to living supernaturally in everyday life	A 12-area spiritual clarity assessment to track real growth	Daily breakthrough habits that shift your words, mindset, and results

Ideal for hungry believers, leaders, and business owners who know there is more — and are ready to walk in it.

Mentored by David Martin, featured on Sid Roth's "It's Supernatural!"

LivingSupernaturally.com

www.ingramcontent.com/pod-product-compliance
Lightning Source LLC
LaVergne TN
LVHW100527110826
845146LV00002B/806

9798994809860